THE
HISTORY
OF THE
WORLD
IN 100
ANIMALS

SIMON BARNES

ILLUSTRATED BY
FRANN PRESTON-GANNON

SIMON & SCHUSTER
London   New York   Sydney   Toronto   New Delhi

CONTENTS

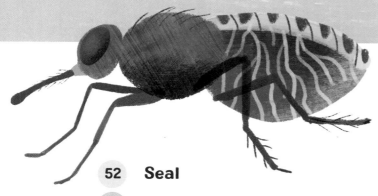

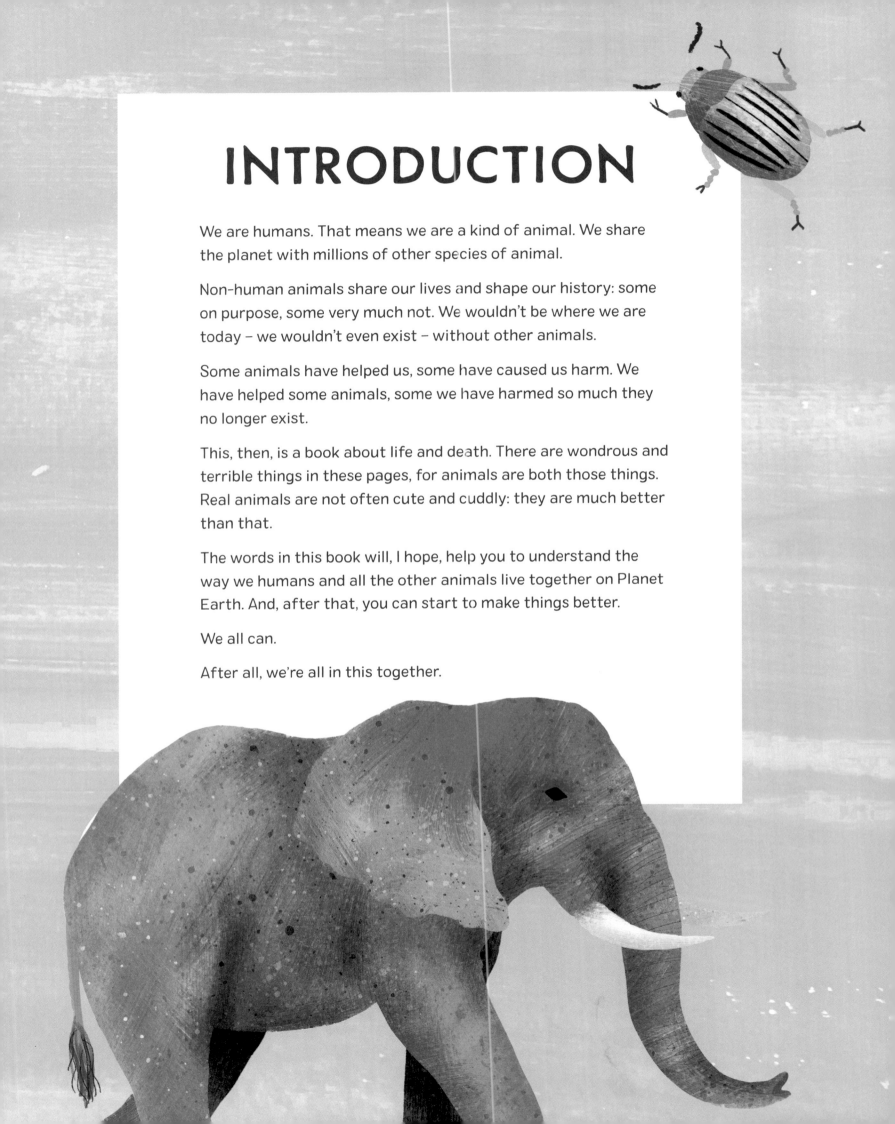

INTRODUCTION

We are humans. That means we are a kind of animal. We share the planet with millions of other species of animal.

Non-human animals share our lives and shape our history: some on purpose, some very much not. We wouldn't be where we are today – we wouldn't even exist – without other animals.

Some animals have helped us, some have caused us harm. We have helped some animals, some we have harmed so much they no longer exist.

This, then, is a book about life and death. There are wondrous and terrible things in these pages, for animals are both those things. Real animals are not often cute and cuddly: they are much better than that.

The words in this book will, I hope, help you to understand the way we humans and all the other animals live together on Planet Earth. And, after that, you can start to make things better.

We all can.

After all, we're all in this together.

1 LION

Let's start with **footprints**. They were made in Africa four million years ago: two living creatures walking together. What kind of animals were these? One adult, one young.
They were **humans** – and they were almost certainly walking hand in hand. When human parents want to keep their child safe from danger – perhaps when crossing a busy road – they say, 'Hold my hand'. But what danger could have faced these humans all those years ago?

Lions.

Lions once lived in Europe, but as the number of humans increased, there was less room for lions. Now you can only find lions in Africa and India.

Lions live in groups called prides. The boss female is in charge of hunting, and the other females do most of the work.

Male lions have huge manes that look like crowns. Lions are **strong** and **fierce**: brave as a lion, we say. Many kings were named after lions, including Richard the Lionheart of England.

The coats of arms of England, Scotland, Canada, Finland, Denmark, Kenya and Montenegro all feature lions.

The first humans walked on two legs on the African plain and they walked with lions. Lions were the **top** animals. They killed and ate other animals to stay alive – including humans. The oldest part of our brain has never forgotten this.

Humans saw lions as their enemies. Early humans lived in **fear** of lions. But many years later, people began hunting lions for sport.

Things began to change about 60 years ago, when people began to worry about what we were doing to all the animals in the world, the non-human animals. People began to change their minds about lions, and about other wild animals. Wouldn't it be better to live in **peace** with each other?

George and Joy Adamson lived in Africa and reared an orphaned lion cub to a fully grown lioness. Her name was Elsa. Pictures of Elsa living in peace with her human friends went around the world. It wasn't as beautiful and peaceful as it seemed. One of Elsa's cubs grew up half-wild, half-tame. He **killed** a man and was later shot.

These days you don't often find lions outside the national parks of Africa and the Gir Forest National Park in India.

There are not as many lions as there were in Elsa's day. Their numbers have dropped 30 per cent in the last 20 years. Now there are only about **20,000** African lions left in the wild. They are classified as **Vulnerable**.

There are four bronze lion statues in Trafalgar Square, London. We like to believe that lions are brave and heroic – that's why they were chosen to guard **Nelson's Column** – a monument to Admiral Horatio Nelson.

130 years ago, when people were building a railway line from Kenya to Uganda, two lions killed around 135 people over two years.

Lions often appear in books and poems. In *The Lion, the Witch and the Wardrobe*, a lion appears as a god-like character.

2 DOMESTIC CAT

The biggest change in human history took place around 12,000 years ago. Instead of looking for plants in the wild, people started to **grow** them. Instead of hunting animals, people kept them at home. People became **farmers**.

They harvested corn and kept it safe for when they needed it. But the corn soon attracted mice and rats, and before long **wild cats** came to feed on the mice and rats.

But cats always push their luck. They came into the places where humans ate and slept. Why didn't they throw them out? Because cats have a secret weapon.

Purring.

Humans have always loved a purring cat: it soothes us, calms us, brings us peace. Cats came into our lives and made them **better**.

Many cats have no human homes to go to: there may be 32 million **feral** cats in the USA. In towns, they often live in large groups with a few female cats in charge.

Cats have been popular as pets for thousands of years – partly because they are quite self-sufficient.

For ancient Egyptians cats were **holy** animals. They had a goddess, Bastet, who looked like a cat.

A cat skeleton was found buried with a human in a Neolithic tomb in Cyprus. It is around **9,500** years old.

If you've ever had a cat or spent much time with one, you'll know they are very good at sleeping – they sleep for around **12 to 18 hours** a day.

3 GORILLA

In the early days of the **movies**, a filmmaker wanted to make the fiercest monster ever seen on the screen. He came up with King Kong: a terrifying giant gorilla that stormed through New York and climbed the Empire State Building.

Less than 50 years later, in one of the most influential pieces of **television** ever made, the great broadcaster David Attenborough was filmed playing with gentle wild gorillas in Africa.

Once gorillas were creatures to fear. Now they are creatures that need our protection. Once all of nature was terrifying and dangerous: now it is something we must look after and love.

Gorillas have changed the way we think about the planet we live on, and about the other animals we **share** it with.

Whilst their existence dates back millions of years, scientists have known about gorillas for less than 200 years. They were first discovered in 1847.

The scientist Dian Fossey spent 19 years living with gorillas. She studied them closely and taught us about the way they live. She found out the meaning of the sounds gorillas make. She showed us that gorillas had gentle manners and a strong sense of family.

Humans are closely related to gorillas: we are both different kinds of ape.

Gorillas make and use tools: one gorilla was observed making a bridge from a tree stump.

Gorillas burp when they're happy.

A fully grown male gorilla has pale fur across his shoulders and is called a **silverback**. Gorillas can get quite large – a big male gorilla can reach up to 199 kilograms!

A captive gorilla called Koko learned human **sign language**. Koko even made jokes. One day she tied her handler's shoelaces together and signed, 'Chase me!'

4 MOCKINGBIRD

Mockingbirds changed the way we think about ourselves and about every other animal that ever lived.

That's because when Charles Darwin visited the Galápagos Islands (near South America) in 1835, he looked at the mockingbirds and saw something peculiar.

The mockingbirds that lived on one of the islands were different to those on the island next door. Darwin asked: **Why**?

When Darwin got home, a bird expert told Darwin that the two mockingbirds were completely different – and different to every other kind of mockingbird.

Darwin carried on thinking . . . and thinking. And after over 20 years of thinking he wrote the book that changed the way we all think – **On the Origin of Species**. It showed the way all animals are related and that all animals adapt across time.

For example, if an antelope's food is the leaves of trees, the higher they can reach, the more leaves they can eat. So the antelope with the longest neck will get the most food and most likely **live longer** and have more young. And the young with the longest neck – longer even than its parents – will have an even better chance of survival.

So, after thousands of years and thousands of parents with thousands of young each with a longer neck, you have . . . a **giraffe**.

Many people were shocked and horrified. If giraffes were related to antelopes, could **humans** be related to **monkeys**?

And, of course, the answer was . . . **yes**!

Charles Darwin visited the Galápagos Islands during a five-year expedition in a boat called HMS *Beagle*.

Mockingbirds like to eat fruit, seeds and insects, such as beetles, bees and butterflies.

Remember the name **Charles Darwin** – he'll crop up again later!

There are around 16 species of mockingbird. The **northern mockingbird** can be found in the USA, Canada and Mexico.

5 AMERICAN BISON

200 years ago, there were around 50–60 million buffaloes in North America. 100 years later, there were only 300 in the whole of the USA.

The USA would not be the country it is today without the **near extinction** of the buffalo.

Before European people came to America, Indigenous tribes – especially the Plains Indians – needed buffaloes to live. Buffalo meat was their food and buffalo skin was their clothing and shelter.

Euro-Americans began killing buffaloes – sometimes at the rate of 5,000 a day – which meant the Plains Indians were left with little to eat. This was the Euro-Americans' tactic to stop the Plains Indians fighting back.

Buffaloes are big – their hump is as high off the ground as a tall man. They used to travel in herds across the plains, following the growth of new grass.

1.98 M

Buffaloes lived in huge herds on the land humans now use to grow food for themselves.

Buffaloes were moved into other wild places in North America. There are now around 13,000 wild buffaloes in the world.

William Cody worked for the Kansas Pacific Railroad, finding meat for the workers. In two years, he killed 4,282 buffaloes. They called him **Buffalo Bill**. He later travelled around America and Europe with a show about the Wild West.

In 1902 there were only 25 left in **Yellowstone National Park**, so the managers at Yellowstone bought 21 buffaloes from private owners and reintroduced them to the park. Now there are around 4,600.

In 2016 President Barack Obama made buffaloes the **national** mammal of the USA.

6 ORIENTAL RAT FLEA

Fleas changed human history. In the fourteenth century, they caused millions of people in Europe to die, a time now known as the **Black Death**.

Oriental rat fleas are insects that live by biting rats and drinking their blood. But they are perfectly happy to bite humans as well.

Sometimes the fleas' bodies carry tiny living bacteria that cause disease – and they accidentally pass them on when they bite. When bitten by such a flea, humans can catch a disease called the **plague**. Before we invented modern medicines this often led to death.

Fleas are insects. Like most insects they start as an egg. The adults are small, wingless and brown (the best colour for hiding in fur). They have flat bodies and long hind legs.

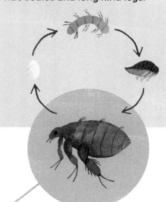

The **plague** begins with shivering, vomiting, headaches and dizziness. It goes on with pain, sleeplessness and swollen lymph nodes.

Back then, no one knew what caused the Black Death. People believed that God was angry, so they went to the Church for help, but the priests couldn't do anything.

An oriental rat flea can **jump** 50 centimetres: 200 times their own body length, like a human jumping over a skyscraper.

After the Black Death, the people who survived saw the world differently – after all, it became obvious that priests weren't as knowledgeable as people had thought they were. So the **Renaissance** began, which was a time of huge change.

There were later outbreaks of plague, but nothing as terrible as the Black Death. There was plague in London only 350 years ago.

People can still get plague, but it is very rare and can now be treated with modern antibiotics.

7 CATTLE

17,000 years ago people painted pictures of aurochs (wild cows or bulls) on the walls of their **caves** because they mattered so much.

Humans hunted them for **food**. This was difficult and dangerous and often the aurochs got away. So people began to keep them near their homes instead.

This too was **difficult** and dangerous: aurochs are strong and fierce and need a lot of food. But now the aurochs were always there when people needed them.

Humans only allowed the nicest, the easiest aurochs to breed and make more aurochs. Over thousands of years, they became easier and easier to look after and became cattle: the cows, bulls and calves we know today.

Many humans still believe that the meat of cattle – **beef** – is the best possible food. Once beef was a treat, but now many people eat it every day.

We have cut down **enormous forests**, which were homes to other animals, to make places where cattle can eat grass.

There are just under **one billion** cattle in the world today. They are farmed for dairy products and meat.

Cows' milk is used to make cheese and butter. The cows' skin is used to make leather for shoes, belts and other items.

Cattle produce a gas called **methane**, which stays in the atmosphere and stops the heat on the planet escaping. Gas from cattle is one of the reasons why the Earth is getting hotter. If we don't stop this happening, all life will be in danger.

8 BLUE WHALE

8

There are more than 30 different kinds of whale. The biggest is the **blue whale** and the smallest is the **dwarf sperm whale**.

Blue whales are the **biggest** animals ever known to have lived – bigger than any dinosaur. They live in the oceans but they breathe air like you and me, because we are both **mammals**.

They can be **30 metres** long and weigh around 170,000 kilograms. A blue whale's heart is as big as a small car. Its tongue is as heavy as a small elephant and its mouth can hold around 90,000 kilograms of food and water.

Blue whales are big, but they're certainly not clumsy. They can move at more than 30 km/h flat out and cruise for miles at 8 km/h.

Blue whales don't have teeth. Their mouths are filled with great hairy sieves called **baleen plates**. They take the world's biggest gulp of krill and seawater and use their huge tongue to push the water back out. The krill are caught on the baleen plates – and become dinner.

You can see – and **hear** – blue whales' great breath from a vast distance across the waves. You can often see a jet of warm air rise up as the whale breathes out of the blowhole on its forehead – it's like having a nose on the top of your head.

Sometimes whales swim on to shore and get stuck. Years ago that was like a mountain of free food to the people who lived nearby.

The blue whale's main food is **krill**. Krill are like shrimps, each one the size of your little finger.

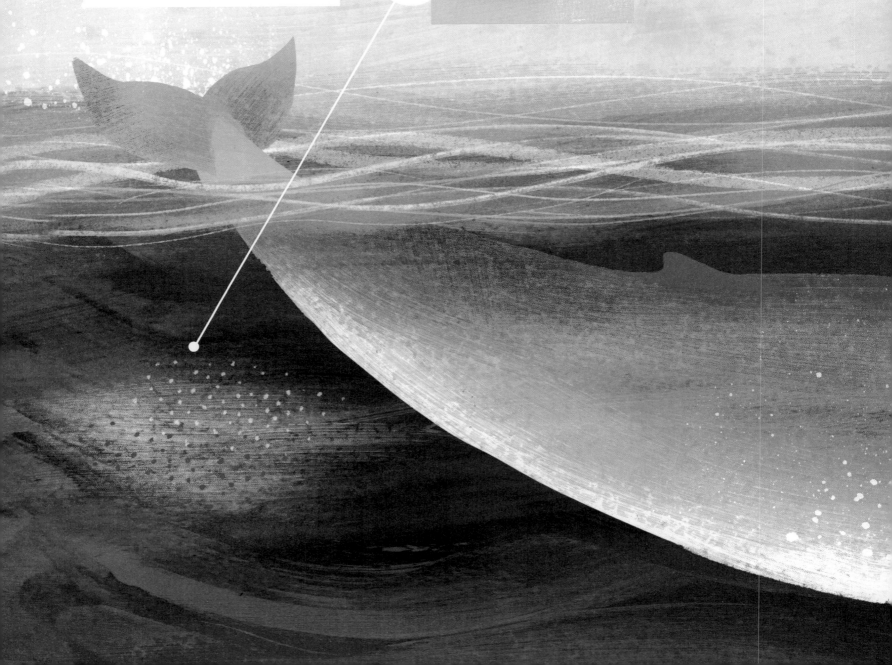

As humans got better with sailing boats, people went to sea to **hunt** whales. They were hunted with a spear called a harpoon.

The meat wasn't all the whalers were after. Whales have a lot of fat – **blubber** – to keep them warm in cold seas. This could be melted down to make oil that was used in lamps.

Light is desperately important for humans. With good lamps humans could live, work, eat and have fun at night. Whale oil helped people see in the darkness.

Then humans invented ships with motors and guns to fire the harpoons. Now it was much easier to hunt whales.

In the first 60 years of the twentieth century, 360,000 blue whales were killed. The blubber wasn't used for lamps anymore, it now had other uses, such as margarine. After that there weren't many blue whales left.

Many people in the world wanted the killing of whales to stop. **'Save the whales!'** More and more people heard those words and agreed with them.

Around 200 years ago, there were about 230,000 blue whales in the Antarctic. There are now less than 25,000 in the whole world.

In 1986 almost every country in the world stopped killing whales – apart from Japan, Norway and Iceland.

It will take the blue whales a long time to recover. But because most humans have stopped hunting them, their numbers are starting to improve.

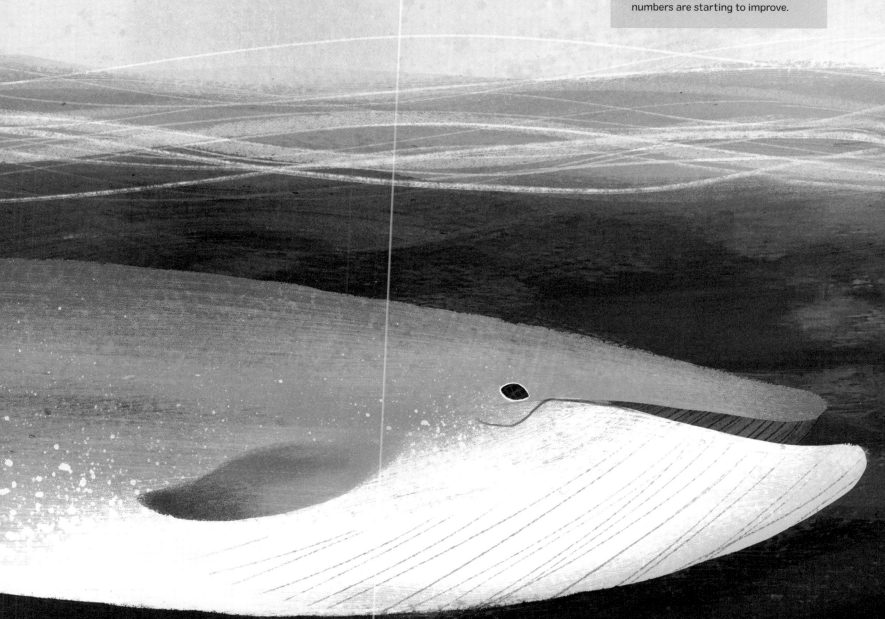

9 CORAL

Coral is the greatest constructor in the animal kingdom – they make islands big enough for humans to live on. 118,000 people live on Kiribati, an island in the Pacific Ocean – and it's essentially an animal.

Corals make a hard skeleton and live inside it. When millions of corals live together, they can create a hard reef – and that can become a decent-sized **island**.

The **Great Barrier Reef** in Australia is 2,000 kilometres long. Famously, you can see it from space.

But as the seas are getting warmer all over the world, the heat is killing corals in many places.

Coral reefs are home to huge numbers of fish and other sea life.

The sea is getting deeper. 530,000 people live on the coral islands of the Maldives, but in 100 years' time, these islands could be underwater.

Corals often live in enormous groups. Some cold-water species have been found at 3,300 metres below sea level.

10 EAGLE

Everybody who sees an eagle wants to be one: big, fierce, beautiful and flying as if it **owned** the whole planet.

Eagles seem to live halfway between us on Earth and the heavens, up in the sky. So eagles are often used to represent **important** people: kings, emperors and gods.

Eagles are national birds of the USA, Zambia, Germany, Mexico and many other countries.

There are not as many eagles in the wild as there used to be, due to hunting and habitat loss. We need to start looking after them.

In the Christian religion, the eagle has often been seen as a bird of God, so you can sometimes spot images of eagles in churches.

Eagles were the badge of the **Roman Empire** 2,000 years ago. They are often used to show the strength of an army. Napoleon Bonaparte and Adolf Hitler both used eagle symbols.

11 PLATYPUS

In 1798 when the first platypus came from Australia to England, many scientists thought it was a practical joke.

It was certainly an odd-looking creature with a beak like a duck, fur like a mole, legs like an otter and a tail like a beaver.

But the platypus wasn't a joke – it was real. You can still find them living in Australia today.

When people first saw this creature, they realised that the planet was much stranger than they had thought.

Platypuses live a semi-aquatic life in the tropical rainforests of Queensland and also in the chilly Tasmanian mountains.

QUEENSLAND

AUSTRALIA

TASMANIA

● PLATYPUS RANGE

Platypuses find their food underwater by detecting little pulses of electricity sent out by the tiny animals they eat. This means they can hunt in complete darkness. Humans couldn't do that in a million years.

Male platypuses have poisonous spikes on their hind legs. They are probably used for fighting other males.

The original platypus skin that was brought back in 1798 still exists and can be found at the Natural History Museum, London.

If you look closely, you can see the marks left by the scissors where scientists tried to prove the beak had been sewn on to the head as a joke.

A platypus is a mammal like us. The females feed their young on milk from their own bodies, like all other mammals. They also lay eggs, like many reptiles, such as lizards, snakes and tortoises. The platypus shows us that reptiles and mammals are related.

12 HONEYBEE

Our ancestors hunted for wild honey made by honeybees as soon as they started to walk across the plains of Africa.

For most people today honey is a treat. But for early humans it was **essential**, as it's high in energy. All this energy fed the human brain. Honey helped our ancestors to think: and thinking is what we humans do best.

As humans got **cleverer**, they started to keep bees at home. Beekeeping is difficult and dangerous – bees sting! – but it was worth the risk. Honey was very important stuff.

There are around **20,000** species of bees worldwide.

Honeybees live together in a hive, which they build in places like hollow trees. In a hive there is a **single queen**, who lays the eggs, thousands of worker bees (all female) and a smaller number of male drones, who fertilise the queen's eggs.

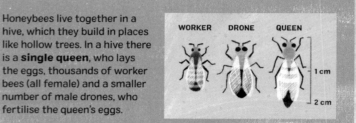

WORKER   DRONE   QUEEN

1 cm

2 cm

Many plants make a sweet juice called nectar. Bees use this to make honey and feed on it during the winter. That's actually good news for the plants – the bees also pick up yellow dust called **pollen** and take it from one flower to another – and that's the way plants make more plants.

700 years ago sugar was only found in Asia; 300 years ago it was still a luxury in most places, so for centuries we needed honeybees and their honey to bring sweetness into our lives.

There are problems for modern honeybees. A hive can collapse and die for reasons we don't really understand. What's more, there are fewer places with wildflowers these days – so it's much harder for bees to find nectar.

13 TYRANNOSAURUS REX

Very big, very fierce and very dead. Well, more than dead actually, **extinct**. *Tyrannosaurus rex* will never walk the Earth again.

T. rex was a dinosaur: and dinosaurs dominated the planet for 150 million years; humans have only been around for 4 million years. *T. rex* was one of the last and the most **fearsome** of them all.

When a great rock from space, called a **meteor**, hit the Earth it killed many of the dinosaurs, including *T. rex.* The shock was bigger than the biggest bomb that ever exploded, and it wiped almost everything out that lived on the planet.

Life on Earth recovered. Big animals once again roamed the planet. But it took an awfully long time.

The discovery of the dinosaurs taught people that the world had been around a lot longer than a few thousand years. The timescale for Planet Earth is now known as **Deep Time** and is roughly about 4.5 billion years.

We are still learning things about *T. rex*. There are still lots of questions to be answered. Was it warm-blooded? Did it have feathers? How fast could it run?

The first *Tyrannosaurus* **teeth** were found in the USA in 1874, and the first skeleton was found in 1902 in Hell Creek, USA.

T. rex is unlike anything alive today. It helps us to understand what extinction really means and the immense changes that have taken place in life on Earth.

In 1905 Henry Fairfield Osborn, president of the American Museum of Natural History, named *Tyrannosaurus rex*, which means **king of the tyrant lizards**.

14 SHARK

If you have ever been to the seaside anywhere in the world, then you have **swum** or paddled with sharks. The sea is full of them: but hardly any of them will do you any harm. There are around 500 species of sharks, some tiny, some huge. But only a small number of species have ever been known to attack a human.

We humans are probably more frightened of sharks than any other creature on the planet. But why? It would make more sense to be scared of cars: far more people die in road accidents than shark attacks. Between 1958 and 2016, 439 people were killed by sharks: less than eight a year in the whole world.

But we are **land** animals. Perhaps we're only truly comfortable on dry land. We have always been a little frightened of the water and what might be **lurking** beneath the surface.

Sharks come in all shapes and sizes. The smallest shark is the **dwarf lantern shark**, which is only about 17 centimetres long. The biggest shark is the **whale shark**, which can be over 12 metres long. They are harmless to humans, but they survive by eating enormous quantities of tiny animals.

The great white shark, tiger shark and bull shark are the most likely to attack humans.

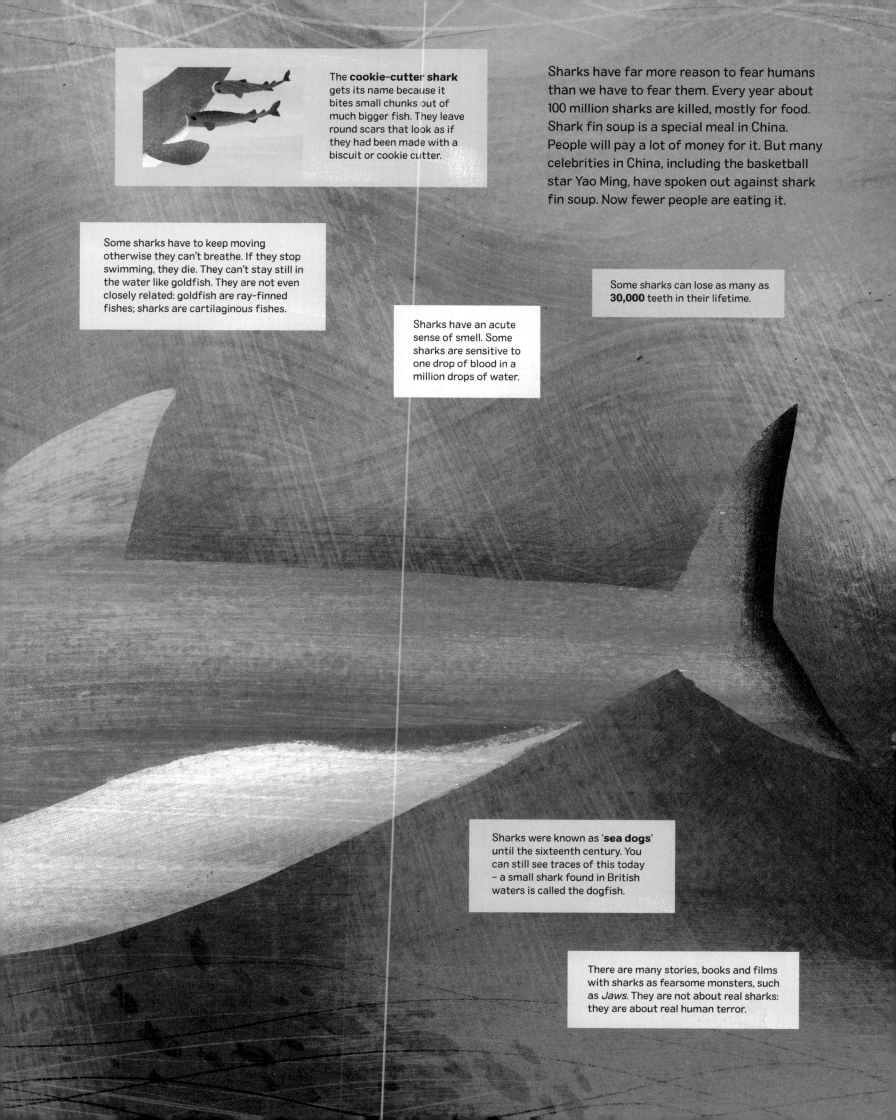

The **cookie-cutter shark** gets its name because it bites small chunks out of much bigger fish. They leave round scars that look as if they had been made with a biscuit or cookie cutter.

Sharks have far more reason to fear humans than we have to fear them. Every year about 100 million sharks are killed, mostly for food. Shark fin soup is a special meal in China. People will pay a lot of money for it. But many celebrities in China, including the basketball star Yao Ming, have spoken out against shark fin soup. Now fewer people are eating it.

Some sharks have to keep moving otherwise they can't breathe. If they stop swimming, they die. They can't stay still in the water like goldfish. They are not even closely related: goldfish are ray-finned fishes; sharks are cartilaginous fishes.

Some sharks can lose as many as **30,000** teeth in their lifetime.

Sharks have an acute sense of smell. Some sharks are sensitive to one drop of blood in a million drops of water.

Sharks were known as '**sea dogs**' until the sixteenth century. You can still see traces of this today – a small shark found in British waters is called the dogfish.

There are many stories, books and films with sharks as fearsome monsters, such as *Jaws*. They are not about real sharks: they are about real human terror.

15 COCKROACH

It's the idea of cockroaches that disgusts us. They make us think that things are **dirty** and that creatures are trying to take over. That's why we dislike them and try to get rid of them.

There may be cockroaches living in your block of flats, your school, even in your favourite restaurant.

Cockroaches can eat almost **anything**: waste human food, fallen hair, flakes of skin, dirty clothes and the droppings of animals.

They keep out of sight, only coming out at night. They are very fast creatures: they can cover 30 centimetres in a second. They can find their way in the dark with long feelers – **antennae**. The fact that you can't see cockroaches doesn't mean they aren't there.

Of the **4,500** different kinds of cockroaches, only four cause problems for humans. They can carry germs that can make people ill. Their droppings can trouble people with asthma and some allergies.

Some cockroaches live and work together, often making decisions as a group. They are clever and complicated animals.

Cockroaches breed at a fast rate, meaning a few cockroaches can become a big **colony** in less than a year.

A cockroach is the only terrestrial animal to have mated in **space** and returned to Earth to produce offspring. Her name was Nadezhda and she was sent into space by Russia in 2007.

Most species of cockroach are great recyclers – often eating the waste that humans leave behind. They play an important part in helping the ecosystems that they inhabit.

16 PANDA

At the beginning of the 1950s many people started to worry that some of our favourite animals might become **extinct**. Top of the worry list was the panda. Pandas were getting rarer and people thought this was because they weren't very good at staying alive.

So they took a number of pandas out of the wild and put them in zoos. A panda called Chi Chi arrived at London Zoo in 1958. In 1966 she was sent to **Moscow** for seven months to meet a male called An An. Everybody hoped they would breed, but they didn't. They only wanted to fight. People thought pandas were a lost cause.

But we know a little better now. We now know that pandas are rare because the bamboo forests where they live were being damaged and **destroyed**.

Humans like pandas because they look cute. But that sweet round head is full of muscles that give them huge biting power.

Pandas live in the forests of China and are **herbivores**. They only eat bamboo – which is a kind of grass.

People are working hard to preserve the natural habitat of the pandas. There are now **40** forest reserves for pandas in China, up from 13 in 1998.

Pandas, like us primates, have a **thumb** for grasping. They use it to hold bamboo. It's not a thumb quite like our own: it's a spur from the wrist bone that does the same job.

THUMB

Pandas may struggle to breed in captivity, but in the wild pandas are actually quite good at breeding.

17 COD

12,000 years ago humans started to keep animals at home instead of hunting them. But not fish. Most of the fish people eat today are still caught in the wild.

Cod has always been a **favourite** of humans, and as we got better and better at catching fish, with bigger boats and huge nets, we started to take too many fish out of the sea.

Atlantic cod can be big (up to 90 kilograms) and they like to swim in deep, cold seas.

There are two species of cod, the **Pacific** and the **Atlantic**. They are related to haddock, whiting and pollock.

12,000 years ago it seemed that nature would feed humans for ever. Now there are many more people in the world, and if we carry on taking fish from the sea as often as we do now, there will be no fish left.

18 EGRET

Many people first got the idea that we are running out of nature because of women's hats.

150 years ago hats were **high fashion** for women, and huge hats were covered in feathers, especially the gorgeous white plumes of egrets, but to get the feathers you had to kill the birds.

Egrets are related to herons: long-necked, long-legged, fish-catching wading birds.

Most egrets are white. In spring they grow especially beautiful plumes. Their feathers were worth their weight in **gold**.

Emily Williamson from Manchester, UK, thought this was a terrible business. So did Harriet Hemenway and Minna B. Hall from Massachusetts, USA. They all started societies to look after the birds. These became known as the **Royal Society for the Protection of Birds** and the **National Audubon Society**.

19 DODO

The dodo was discovered by Europeans in 1598. Around 60 years later, the bird was **extinct**. But nobody noticed. Back then, no one realised that humans could wipe out a whole species.

Dodos only lived on the island of **Mauritius** in the Indian Ocean. They couldn't fly, but it is thought they were **fast runners**.

They had lived successfully on Mauritius for many thousands of years – until the Europeans came and changed everything.

Dodos were big birds around a metre in height and weighing up to 17 kilograms, with a spectacular beak.

No one knows how they got the name 'dodo'. Perhaps it came from the Dutch word **dodoor**, which means sluggish.

The dodo was a rainforest-dwelling bird that fed mostly on fruit, seeds, nuts and roots.

When Europeans arrived and cut down the forests for growing sugar cane, the dodos had nowhere to live. Europeans also introduced rats and other mammals to the island, which ate the dodos' eggs.

20 DONKEY

Donkeys were one of the first animals that humans used for **heavy lifting**. They are much easier to look after than horses, as they are smaller, need less food and they don't mind being on their own.

The donkey was domesticated from the African wild asses that most likely came from Egypt. Today there are more than 40 million donkeys – and fewer than 200 wild asses; donkeys came from wild asses.

Donkeys are used to do some of the dirtiest and **hardest** jobs for humans in the poorest parts of the world. They are often used to carry people and things from place to place.

Donkeys live a **long time** – a donkey can live for 25–30 years. Some have even been known to live into their fifties.

Donkeys and humans have lived together for thousands of years and they feature in many of our myths and stories, including *A Midsummer Night's Dream* by William Shakespeare.

In the UK, donkeys became a holiday treat. Many children rode donkeys on the beach, and in some places you still can.

People love donkeys and there are many charities that look after them. In some countries, charities educate donkey owners and help provide veterinary care.

21 WOLF

When humans became farmers 12,000 years ago, we began to see wolves as our deadly **enemies**. Humans kept sheep for food on their farms, as it was a lot easier than hunting them. Trouble is, it made it easier for wolves too.

Many wolves would enter the farms, killing and scaring the animals. But when humans invented firearms, wolves became very wary of going near the places where humans lived. It was a kind of **war** – and the humans won.

Wolves live in packs and defend their territories fiercely. In most packs only the top (**alpha**) male and the top female have cubs. The others wolves help to raise them.

Wolves still live in the USA and in parts of Europe. In **Yellowstone Park**, USA, wolves have been reintroduced into the wild.

As there were more and more humans in the world, forests and wild places where wolves lived were **destroyed**. Wolves have not been seen in Britain for around 350 years.

Wolves in a pack live very closely together. They understand each other well, and pass on their moods and their ideas. They read each other's faces, just as we do. They keep in touch over long distances by howling.

Many of our oldest stories are about wolves and how scary they are. In *Little Red Riding Hood*, the wolf disguises himself as the girl's grandmother and tries to eat her.

PIGEON/DOVE

We love doves, but we hate pigeons. Doves stand for **peace**, and in the Christian religion they stand for the Holy Spirit . . . but city pigeons are often seen as dirty and disgusting. But they are the same creatures.

Racing pigeons, city pigeons, ornamental white doves all come from the **same** species. They are all descended from the wild species of **rock dove**.

Thousands of years ago, people often used caves for shelter. The rock doves also build their nests in the caves. A young rock dove, or pigeon, needs to be almost **adult-sized** before it can fly, which meant that humans could easily catch a young pigeon just by reaching into a nest. It was an instant meal. Pigeons helped people to stay alive. Humans have been living with rock doves ever since.

Pigeons are **clever**. Scientists have trained them to store a library of 1,000 images in their minds, and they have responded well to tests involving numeracy and literacy.

Pigeons can find their way back home over long distances. They have been used to carry important messages – especially in wartime. 32 pigeons have been awarded the **Dickin Medal** because the messages they carried saved human lives.

People also keep pigeons for their looks, fancy flying, fan-shaped tails and huge throats.

Charles Darwin (**remember him?**) kept pigeons and was fascinated by them. He recognised that if people could change the features of a pigeon in a few years through breeding – then massive changes must have happened in the natural world over thousands of years.

Male and female pigeons love to be together. That's why we say '**lovey-dovey**'.

23 MOSQUITO

Mosquitoes are responsible for the deaths of many people. It's been suggested that half the humans that have ever lived have died from mosquito bites. At least 500,000 people still die every year from mosquitoes.

Like fleas, mosquitoes drink **blood**. They can carry tiny but dangerous living things in their bodies and pass them on when they bite.

Malaria is one of the diseases that mosquitoes can carry. It causes a high fever, hot sweats and, sadly, many people die from it.

Malaria has been a problem for humans ever since we started to become **farmers**, living in one place rather than wandering and following the food. People living in the same place make an easy target.

There are around 3,500 kinds of mosquitoes, but not all of them bite humans. Their name comes from the Spanish word '**mosca**' and means '**little fly**'.

Mosquitoes can sense your body heat and the **carbon dioxide** you breathe out from 30 metres away.

Only **female** mosquitoes bite. They need the blood to lay their eggs.

Humans didn't realise that malaria came from mosquitoes until the late nineteenth century. Once we found out, we did all we could to get rid of them. We invented a chemical called **DDT** that killed the mosquitoes, but it also killed lots of other insects that are important for humans. Many countries banned DDT.

Mosquitoes lay their eggs in stagnant water, and when the larvae hatch they live in the water, eating tiny particles of food.

24 TIGER

For the past 50 years we have been trying to make sure that tigers don't become extinct. At the beginning of the **twentieth century** there were 100,000 tigers in the world, but now there are less than 4,000.

Though there is some good news: tiger numbers are stable, perhaps even increasing in some areas. That's because people love tigers and have worked hard to save them. We admire their **beauty** and their **fierce** nature. Most people think that the world needs tigers. If we let tigers become extinct, we will feel we have failed. The best way to save them is to look after the wild places where they live.

Tigers were once found all across Central Asia, Mongolia, South and South East Asia, and up into Siberia. These days they are mainly found in **India**, **China** and **Siberia**.

Tigers don't work together in a pack like lions. Tigers hunt alone. They mostly live alone too, though a mother stays with her cubs until they are big enough to hunt for themselves.

Tigers try to stay away from people, as they know people have fires and weapons. However, this is not always the case as the **Champawat Tiger of Nepal** killed (or so it's believed) 436 people before she was shot in 1907.

Tigers have been admired throughout history and in many different cultures. The Hindu warrior goddess Durga rides a tiger. In **Buddhism**, the tiger represents anger and there are traditions of 'were-tigers' (men who turn into tigers) in India, Malaysia and Indonesia. William Blake's famous poem 'The Tyger' celebrates the tiger for being fierce.

There are three big illegal trades in the world. These involve **guns**, **drugs** and **wild animals**. Sometimes animals are bought and sold alive, sometimes it's their dead bodies, and sometimes it's just parts of their bodies, such as their skins or bones. People have traded tigers for centuries. They still do – even though it's now against the law all over the world.

Tigers ambush their prey by hiding and sneaking up close. Then, when they are very close indeed, they pounce.

The Romans kept tigers to entertain people in circuses and to show off. Many people still like to keep tigers as pets. There are probably more tigers in Texas, USA, than there are in India.

25 RAT

Humans don't like being compared to rats – it's actually one of the worst **insults** you can come up with. It means you think that a person is nasty and **cunning**.

But we are actually quite a lot like rats. We share **90 per cent** of our DNA – the stuff we get from our parents when we are born – with rats, so they are often used to test important human medicines. If it makes rats better, then it will probably make people better.

There are more than **60 species** of rat, but the two that can be found living with humans are the brown rat and the black rat. They are very clever indeed at living with us and eating the food that we collect for ourselves and our domestic animals.

Rats live with humans all over the world, in big cities and farmland, but we don't often see them. They are very good at keeping out of sight.

Rats soil food, carry disease and leave droppings. They can also carry **fleas** that can be dangerous to humans.

Rats are rodents. The big teeth at the front of their mouths never stop growing, so they never wear out. Rats are brilliant at gnawing.

Scientists keep rats in **laboratories** for many different kinds of experiments. Thanks to rats, we have learned many important things about **cancer**, and even how to cure certain cancers.

Rats have also been used to study **intelligence**. The cleverest rats tend to have the cleverest babies – showing us that intelligence is inherited from your parents.

Where humans travelled, rats often went with them. The rats we took to **remote islands** often ate the eggs and young of seabirds.

26 WASP

Wasps are famous for spoiling picnics. But if it wasn't for wasps, you wouldn't be holding this book in your hands.

Some kinds of wasps live, work, eat and breed together. To do that, they need a base. A home. And so they make one. **A nest**. A wasp's nest is a lovely thing: incredibly light and so neat it is almost perfect.

A wasp's nest is made from **paper**. To make their nest they chew wood, spit it out and from the squashy mess they make . . . paper. Around 2,000 years ago, people in China noticed this and started to make paper for themselves.

Wasps have been around since the time of the **dinosaurs**. Their ancestors are over 200 million years old.

The smallest wasp is the **fairy wasp**, which is no bigger than 0.14 millimetres, and the largest is the **Asian giant hornet**, which can grow to 5 centimetres long.

People in China started to use paper for **writing** and **drawing**. Facts, ideas and beliefs could be written down and passed from one person to another. Paper was such marvellous stuff it soon started to spread across the world. Paper was a much bigger **invention** than the internet.

There are more than 30,000 species of wasps and many of them are **solitary**. The social species of wasps live in communities that share the important jobs, such as breeding or caring for young.

Most wasps tend to be black and yellow, which is a **danger** sign to predators. They are saying: don't attack me, you'll regret it.

27 EARTHWORM

Next time you see a worm in a garden, remember to say thank you. Without earthworms life on Earth would be very different.

All life on land goes back to the **soil**. It begins with the plants that grow in the soil: and the soil is what it is because of earthworms. They take in soil at one end of their bodies and pass it out at the other, taking out tiny **particles** of food as they do so. This changes the nature of the soil and makes it richer, which is much better for growing plants.

The forests across the world and the fields where we grow our food are what they are because of the actions of the earthworms below the ground.

There are 6,000 different kinds of earthworms. In a hectare of healthy soil, there can be as many as a million worms.

Every earthworm is a **hermaphrodite** – which means they are both male and female.

They move by lengthening and shortening their bodies through the earth, a process called **peristalsis**.

Many modern farming methods are not good for worms. Deep ploughing damages worm tunnels and chemicals **destroy** the worms' food. This may cause serious damage over time and no one knows how soil would work without worms.

Earthworms don't have eyes, but they have **photosensitive** cells, which means daylight is their enemy.

28 SNAKE

There are around 3,600 different kinds of snakes and about 375 of them are poisonous – or rather **venomous**. Poison does you harm when you eat or drink it; venom does you harm when it gets into your blood.

Snakes put venom into blood by biting. That's how they hunt: they hide, they **bite** and what they bite they eat. There's no point in biting humans: humans are much too big for venomous snakes to eat.

But snakes also bite when they think they're in danger – and that's when humans can get hurt. 250 kinds of snakes can kill a human with a single bite and around 100,000 people a year die from a snakebite.

Most snakes have **no eyelids** and no ears that you can see. They use their tongues to smell; that's why they flicker in and out. They are very sensitive to vibrations and some snakes can see in the dark like an **infrared** camera.

Snakes have several different ways of moving – and they all look spooky to humans. The one they use most – slithering along in curves – is called **lateral undulation**.

Their long, thin shape makes snakes very good at keeping out of sight. That's why they are good hunters.

In many stories, myths and legends, snakes are shown as evil and untrustworthy. In the Bible, the devil appears as a snake. Snakes are hated and feared all over the world.

Some non-venomous snakes kill by crushing their prey to death. In 2017 the body of an adult human was found inside a seven-metre python. The human had been crushed and swallowed whole.

29 CHICKEN

The red jungle fowl is a colourful bird once found only in the forests of Asia. But now you can find them all over the world. Around 8,000 years ago, humans began **domesticating** them and they are now known as chickens.

You can keep them very easily, so long as you have a little space. The females – hens – lay eggs, and both male and female birds can be kept for meat.

A chicken kept in good conditions with space to move about, a place to **roost** for the night and decent food can easily live five years. But many chickens are now kept in battery farms. Here they live in very small, cramped spaces and can't move. They often only live a few weeks. This is a way of producing a lot of chickens to keep up with the demands of humans. But many people now see battery farms as cruel and are choosing to eat free-range chickens and eggs instead.

Chicken was once a treat that humans would enjoy occasionally. But now people are overindulging in foods, including chicken, which is leading to many **health problems** for humans, but also for chickens.

A chicken used to mean a young bird that had just hatched, but we now use the word to describe all the birds (hens and roosters), as well as the meat.

A male chicken under a year old is called a **cockerel**. After that they are called **roosters**.

MONKEY

All humans are related to each other. If you and I went back through our families for many generations, we would find someone we share – a **relation** to us both.

All humans are also related to monkeys. If you and I invited a monkey to join us at looking at our ancestors, we would have to go back a lot further – but in the end, going back millions of years, we would find a relative that all three of us shared.

Charles Darwin wrote two books that showed how we are related to monkeys. He said he was proud to be related to 'a **heroic** little monkey'.

There are about 260 different kinds of monkeys and most of them live in trees. The smallest monkey is known as the **pygmy marmoset** and is about 12 centimetres long and the largest is the **mandrill** (famous for its rainbow bottom), which can reach about a metre in length and weigh over 36 kilograms.

Monkeys have eyes that face forward, like ours. This helps them to see very clearly as they jump from branch to branch.

In the late 1940s, a monkey called Albert was sent into **space** in a rocket to see if humans could survive out there. Sadly, the experiment was not a success and Albert died.

Monkeys have hands with **thumbs** that point the opposite way to their fingers (just like us). These help them grab food and branches. Hands with thumbs are also useful when using and making tools. When our **ancient relatives** started to walk on the ground instead of climbing trees, their hands helped them find food and make shelters.

Monkeys are separated into two categories: Old World and New World. Old World monkeys live in Asia and Africa, while New World monkeys live in the Americas.

31 ARCHAEOPTERYX

Many people hated Charles Darwin's big idea – the **theory of evolution** by natural selection. They didn't want to be related to monkeys. They wanted him to be wrong.

So they asked: if creatures evolved over **Deep Time**, as Darwin had said, there must be something halfway. Where are the in-betweeners? The half-and-halfers? But there weren't any obvious examples, so people said Darwin must be wrong.

He wasn't. And in 1861, just two years after his book, *On the Origin of Species,* was published, a fossil was found in Germany. The creature had teeth and claws. But it also had wings and feathers. Was it a bird? Was it a dinosaur?

Well, actually it was both. It was called **archaeopteryx** and it was the perfect in-betweener.

Archaeopteryx could fly, though not brilliantly.

More archaeopteryx fossils have been found since 1861.

32 HOUSEFLY

Flies annoy us, but they are also one of the most brilliant flying creatures on the entire planet.

They have marvellous eyes that allow them to understand the space around them. They can land on the ceiling by performing a **half-roll**.

Most insects have four wings, but flies have two. Their rear wings have become **halteres**, tiny moving organs that allow the fly to understand exactly where it is in the air.

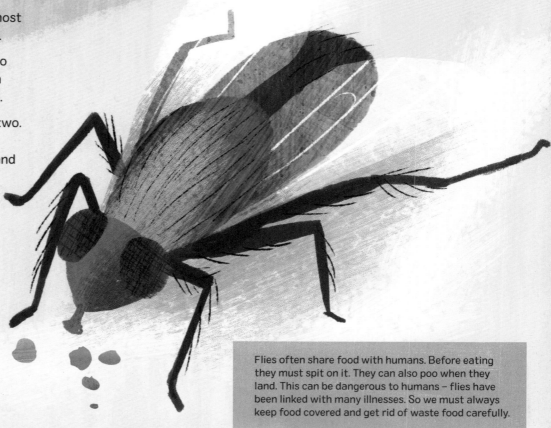

Flies can beat their wings 200–300 times per second and they travel at around 7.2 km/h.

Houseflies taste food using special organs on their feet.

Flies often share food with humans. Before eating they must spit on it. They can also poo when they land. This can be dangerous to humans – flies have been linked with many illnesses. So we must always keep food covered and get rid of waste food carefully.

33 DOG

It you go back through any dog's family far enough (a good few thousand years) you will find a wolf.

When humans started to become farmers 12,000 years ago, wolves took to visiting their villages in search of a free meal from the rubbish humans left around.

Humans soon learned that wolves were quite helpful. They made **warning noises** when enemies were near, just as dogs do now. They could also help humans hunt, as they could find animals with their brilliant sense of **smell**.

So humans started to breed the nicest, gentlest wolves together to make pet dogs.

Dogs can be huge: a large **English mastiff** can weigh 155 kilograms, but a **Yorkshire terrier** only weighs up to 3.2 kilograms.

It's estimated there are about **900 million** dogs in the world.

People only began having dogs in their homes about 80 years ago. Before that they were mostly kept in kennels outside.

Dogs can be trained to help blind and deaf people. They can also learn to sniff out weapons and explosives.

Dogs have appeared in stories and art for thousands of years, such as Toto in *The Wonderful Wizard of Oz* by L. Frank Baum, Jip in *David Copperfield* by Charles Dickens, and Snowy in the *Tintin* cartoons by Hergé.

34 BEAR

Bears have sharp claws and teeth. They can run faster than you, but don't bother climbing a tree to escape. They can climb better than you as well.

Bears are **fierce** animals and they can kill people. So why do parents give their children teddy bears – often as their very first toy?

We like bears because they are a bit like us. They can stand on their hind legs; they have round heads and round faces. Like us – but unlike most other mammals – they walk with their heels flat on the ground. This is called **plantigrade locomotion**.

There are **eight** different kinds of bears. They are: panda, polar bear, American black bear, Asian black bear, sun bear, sloth bear, spectacled bear and the brown or grizzly bear.

The **European** brown bear and the **American** grizzly bear are the same species.

Bears have been trained to dance. Well, not really dancing. You train the bear by making it stand on hot metal, so it has to keep moving its paws. Dancing bears are now banned in most countries, as it is a cruel practice.

In parts of Asia, some people think that bear **bile**, which comes from a bear's liver, is good medicine. There are even farms for bears so that people can get this valuable stuff.

From the sixteenth century until the nineteenth century, people used to catch bears and then make a public show by setting dogs on them. This was called **bear-baiting**.

How did bears come to be the world's favourite toy? It all began with Theodore Roosevelt. He was a president of the USA (1901–1909) and his nickname was . . . **Teddy**.

Teddy loved hunting and had shot a lot of bears. But then a story got out: he had refused to shoot an American black bear cub. People liked the idea of this soft-hearted president. There was even a newspaper drawing of him refusing to shoot this adorable bear cub. Then an American toy designer came up with the idea of the toy bear. He called it 'Teddy's bear'. Now the world is full of **teddy bears**.

Toy bears look much cuter than real bears, with big eyes and flat faces.

Bears rarely attack humans. They kill about two people a year in the USA – usually when they've been startled.

Humans have always had a close **connection** with bears. We even use a lot of names that mean bear, including Arthur, Bernard, Auberon and Ursula.

There are many lovable bears in children's books, including A. A. Milne's **Winnie-the-Pooh** and Michael Bond's **Paddington**.

35 CAMEL

Camels can look a bit odd in Europe or America, where it's hard to see the point of them. You need to see them in the desert.

Their **humps** are full of fat and act like a backpack filled with energy. This means a camel can walk across a desert without needing any water for ten days, longer if they can find fresh green leaves.

Camels have two-toed feet that spread out wide. One reason for this is so that they can walk comfortably on dry sand – anyone who has been to the seaside knows how hard that can be.

There are **three** kinds of camels. The **dromedary** has one hump and was found originally in North Africa and West Asia. The **domestic** and the **wild Bactrian camels** have two humps and live mainly in Central Asia (though you may see them in Australia because people took camels there and some of them went wild).

The wild Bactrian camel is found in the Gobi and the Taklamakan Deserts. There are only around **950 camels** left in the wild and they are classified as **Critically Endangered**.

Humans have kept camels for thousands of years. They are used for meat and milk and their hides can be used to make tents.

Camels allow humans to travel across the desert. A camel can carry a rider around 50 kilometres in a day.

Camels are **highly social** animals and tend to live together in herds.

36 PENGUIN

Penguins charm us, they delight us and they make us laugh. They look clumsy and awkward when they walk. But when they reach the water, they swim like **underwater rockets**, sleek, swift and certain.

Penguins first came to zoos in the middle of the nineteenth century – and they were a **sensation**. People loved the comedy of their walk – and the way it was followed by such graceful swimming. Every zoo had to have penguins.

Television later brought penguins into our sitting rooms. In 1995 the documentary *March of the Penguins* was a global hit. Penguins have taught us about the wonderful strangeness of wildlife all over the world.

There are about 18 species of penguin. The biggest is the **emperor penguin**, who march over 100 kilometres to the sea to catch fish for their newly hatched chicks.

Emperor penguins spend the winter in the coldest place on Earth – Antarctica – where it can be -40 °C. They can dive more than **500 metres** deep and stay under the water for around 20 minutes.

Penguins can't fly – at least not through the air. But their wings are perfect for flying underwater. Most species can cruise in the water at around 11 km/h.

Many species of penguin are declining, with five species currently listed as **Endangered**.

In 1932 a food company started selling a biscuit called **Penguin**. Soon it was a popular treat. Three years later, a company wanted to sell serious books in a friendly way – so they called the books Penguins.

37 OCTOPUS

For centuries humans have been fascinated by the idea of **intelligent** creatures that look nothing like us. Again and again, when we imagine some kind of frightening super-smart alien we come up with something like an octopus.

The more we study real octopuses, the more we learn about how clever they are. Fishermen have always known that octopuses are pretty smart. They can climb into – and out of – lobster pots, eating the lobsters before the fishermen can get to them. They have also been known to climb on to fishing boats in search of food.

They have been studied in tanks in laboratories and can complete complicated **mazes**. They have good memories and can watch a task, copy it and use this new skill to find food.

There are about 300 different species of octopus. The **giant Pacific octopus** can stretch its tentacles 4.3 metres. But some smaller species can only manage 3 centimetres.

For an invertebrate octopuses have large brains compared to the size of their bodies, and this usually means **intelligence**.

Octopuses are clever like humans, but they aren't even closely related to us. They are in a **phylum** (group) called **Mollusca** – which means they are related to slugs and snails. We are in a phylum called **Chordata** – creatures with backbones. Octopuses show us that a creature from another phylum can be every bit as smart as those of us that have backbones. In some cases, even smarter.

Octopuses have been seen playing. An octopus in a tank used the air-flow system to squirt a small bottle about the tank. Some octopuses kept in tanks have been known to climb out and visit their neighbours in different tanks.

Octopus-like creatures play an important part in many myths and legends from different cultures. The Greeks had **Medusa**, a Gorgon with snakes in her hair who looked like an octopus. They also invented **Scylla**, a kind of super-octopus with 12 feet and 6 heads, each head on a long snake-like neck. Scylla ate six sailors in the great epic *The Odyssey*.

The first invented monsters from space were like octopuses. In *The War of the Worlds* by H. G. Wells, published in 1898, the Martians invade Earth and have tentacles like an octopus.

The British sci-fi series *Doctor Who* has a race called the **Ood**. They are basically an octopus in a suit. In this series, the Doctor has two hearts. A real octopus has three.

Octopuses have two eyes, a beak and a mouth at the centre of their eight limbs.

38 DOLPHIN

Humans have always liked and admired dolphins. Dolphins live in water, but they are **mammals** like us, so they must come to the surface to breathe.

They are clever and love to play. They ride with ships for the fun of it. They can jump clear of the water, and it looks as if they are jumping for joy. Dolphins have also shown very **high intelligence** in scientific tests. They are so clever that many people now think it's wrong to keep dolphins in captivity.

There are many stories of dolphins **helping** humans in trouble at sea, and some of them are true. Sometimes dolphins and humans have even fished together.

There are about 30 species of dolphin, including the **common bottlenose dolphin**. Every bottlenose dolphin has a personal sound, or whistle. It's like their name.

Dolphins find their prey by using sound: they emit loud clicks though a fatty organ in the head called a **melon** and listen to the echoes. This gives them a sound picture of their world.

Dolphins off the coast of Australia teach their young how to use a piece of **sponge** to protect their sensitive noses while looking for food on the bottom of the sea.

Dolphins can get caught in fishing nets that stop them getting to the surface to breathe, causing them to drown.

Dolphins are so clever that some scientists have wondered if they have an idea about what's **right** and what's **wrong**, like we do.

Dolphins are fast and agile swimmers. Bottlenose dolphins can travel at speeds of over 40 km/h.

39 RHINOCEROS

Many animals are struggling to survive because humans have damaged the places where they live – this is called **habitat destruction**.

Africa still has suitable habitat for rhinoceroses, but there are hardly any of them living in it. That's because people hunt and kill them to make medicines. Some people believe that rhino horn can help with problems of the blood, headaches and even cancer.

Rhino horn is made from **keratin**, the same material as your fingernails. However, scientific tests have proved that rhino horn isn't very good medicine. But despite this many people still believe it works – so rhinos are killed, and their horns sold. It's against the law, but people can make a lot of money.

Three out of the five species of rhino are **Critically Endangered**. There are currently only around 60 Javan rhinos left in the wild.

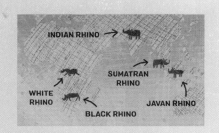

INDIAN RHINO

SUMATRAN RHINO

WHITE RHINO

JAVAN RHINO

BLACK RHINO

There are five species of rhino: two in Africa and three in Asia. The **black rhino** and the **white rhino** are African. Oddly, both are actually grey. In Asia you can find the **Indian**, the **Sumatran** and the **Javan** rhino.

Sometimes wild rhinos have their horns sawn off. The idea is that it will save them from people who want to kill them just for their horns.

In the 1960s serious efforts were made to keep wild rhinos safe. Rhinos have been put back into areas where they used to live, but it's very difficult and expensive.

Rhinoceros comes from Greek words meaning **'nose-horn'**.

40 NIGHTINGALE

Music depends on two things: **rhythm**, which makes you want to tap your feet, and **melody**, which makes you want to sing.

We learn about rhythm before we are born. We spend our first nine months inside our mothers, listening to her heartbeat. But melody we've learned from birds.

Nightingales are some of the greatest of all bird **singers**. They have one of the most complicated songs of all birds. A bird can make more than **600 different sounds** and put them together in 250 different groups.

So when the first humans sang, they had the rhythm they got from their mothers and the melody they borrowed from the birds.

We have only been able to listen to **recorded music** for 100 years or so. Before that if you wanted music you had to make your own or listen to the birds.

The first musical instruments were **flutes**: people made them from bone and they sounded like birds. The oldest flute is 43,000 years old.

Only male nightingales sing. They sing first to find a female and then to protect their nests from other nightingales.

Nightingales are birds that migrate. This means they spend their summers in Europe and West Asia, getting as far north as southern England, and in the winter they go to Africa to find warmer weather.

Nightingales sing in the day as well as at night. On a still evening you can hear a nightingale **two kilometres** away.

41 PIG

We often use the term 'pig' as an insult, even though pigs are one of the most important animals that humans have ever **domesticated**. They were domesticated from a species that we call wild boar.

Around 12,000 years ago, our ancestors probably kept herds of pigs, following them, feeding them and getting them used to humans.

They are easy to keep because they'll eat almost anything, and it's often been said that you can eat all of a pig except its **squeak**. Although in some religions, eating pork is strictly forbidden.

Pigs are lively, **intelligent** creatures that love to be together. People who look after pigs often like them a lot.

Pigs roll in mud to protect their skin from heat, flies and the cold.

There were wild pigs in the UK around 400 years ago. About 25 years ago, there was a craze for eating the meat of wild pigs in restaurants, so they were kept on special farms. Sometimes they escaped, and now there are wild pigs back in the UK.

There are many **lovable** pig characters in books and films, including Miss Piggy from Jim Henson's *The Muppets* and Wilbur from *Charlotte's Web* by E. B. White.

Pigs need lots of water. They can drink at least **13 litres** a day.

42 CHIMPANZEE

You have a code inside you. You can find it in every part of your body. It's the instructions for making you. We call this code **DNA**.

You share some of your DNA with everyone you are related to. You get half your DNA from your mother and the other half from your father, but unless you are an **identical** twin no one has exactly the same DNA as you.

The DNA you share shows how closely you are related to someone else. And you share around **98 per cent** of your DNA with chimpanzees.

Chimpanzees are more closely related to humans than they are to gorillas. We have always found chimpanzees fascinating and troubling.

Young chimpanzees have an intense and long bond with their mother. They stay together for up to **seven** years.

Chimpanzees and bonobos live in Africa. Like us, their network of friends and relations are very important to them.

CHIMPANZEES
GORILLAS
BONOBOS

Chimpanzees are a versatile species. They can make their homes on the savannah, in deep rainforest and in dry woodland. They eat many different kinds of foods, but **fruit** is the most important.

Many chimpanzees seem to quarrel a lot, but they also make up a lot. Falling out and making up again is part of chimpanzee life.

Chimpanzees have been taught to use the **sign languages** that were invented for deaf people. Washoe was a chimpanzee who learned 350 different signs. He once signed, 'You me go out.' His teacher signed back, 'OK, but put clothes on.' Washoe at once put on his jacket.

In 1960 Jane Goodall went to Gombe Stream National Park in Tanzania, Africa, to study chimpanzees. She sat and she watched, and she learned and she made notes. She discovered things that changed the way we humans understand chimpanzees and ourselves.

She saw a chimpanzee – who she called David Greybeard – using a **tool**. He took a stick to fetch insects from a hole so he could eat them. People thought that humans were the only animals ever to use a tool. It was a discovery that shocked the world. Later, she saw David Greybeard working with another stick to make it the right length and shape for fetching more insects.

Jane showed us that chimpanzees are far more **complicated** than we had thought and far more like humans than we believed possible.

Chimpanzees are very social animals. The use their facial expressions, body language and voice to communicate – just like us.

43 ALBATROSS

At the bottom of the world lies the continent of **Antarctica**. All the way round it, with no land at all to get in the way, is the Southern Ocean. Not many humans go there, but those that do are amazed by the albatrosses they see.

Wandering albatrosses have immense wings: sometimes 3.5 metres from wingtip to wingtip. They barely flap their wings, **gliding** and soaring through the air instead. In the strong winds of the Southern Ocean they can fly for hours, looking for food, without flapping or getting tired.

Humans have always loved albatrosses: written poems about them, made up stories about them and wanted to fly in the same way.

There are around **22 species** of albatross. They mainly live out on the ocean, only coming to land to breed.

Many species of albatross have been under threat from human activity. Albatrosses can get caught on **fishing hooks** and drown. Also, when humans arrived, they accidentally brought rats and mice with them to the remote islands, which ate albatross eggs and chicks.

Many people are now trying to save the albatross by altering their fishing methods and clearing the islands of rodents. In 2018 the island of **South Georgia** in the South Atlantic was cleared of rats and mice – for the first time in 250 years.

The television programme *Blue Planet II* showed albatrosses feeding bits of **plastic** to their chicks, which can kill them. Many people were horrified and decided to use less plastic.

Albatrosses can live for a very long time. They can live for up to 50 years.

44 PASSENGER PIGEON

Humans killed passenger pigeons and destroyed their habitats for food and to protect their crops.

200 years ago there were more passenger pigeons than any other kind of bird that has ever existed. 100 years later they were **extinct**, and humans did it.

Passenger pigeons lived in North America in numbers that are almost impossible to imagine. There was once a flock 1.5 kilometres wide and **480 kilometres** long. It took 14 hours to pass overhead and had in it – so far as anyone could guess – around 3.5 billion birds.

There are more than 300 species of pigeon still living. But this doesnt make up for the loss of the passenger pigeon.

The last passenger pigeon died in **Cincinnati Zoo** in 1914. Her name was Martha.

45 TSETSE FLY

Adult tsetse flies must have a blood meal every day. They live in **Africa** and they bite humans. They also bite domestic animals: cows, goats and donkeys. They carry dangerous things in their saliva that can cause **illness** and death.

In many parts of Africa, where you find the tsetses, you can't keep domestic animals for food or to help with the heavy work of farming, because the tsetses bite them and they get ill and die. So people have to do the work by hand.

Tsetse flies give people **sleeping sickness**, and you can die from it unless you get treatment. Before 1970 many people became sick with it, but since medicine became available these numbers have fallen. In 2009 for the first time there were fewer than 10,000 reported cases.

Unlike mosquitoes, both male and female tsetse flies drink blood, but it is mainly the male that bites humans.

Humans have kept away from places with the most tsetse flies. These places are now the great national parks of Africa, which are full of lions, elephants and giraffes.

46 DUCK

There are more than 150 species of duck, but we have only domesticated two of them: the **Muscovy duck** of Mexico and South America and the **mallard**, which can be found all over the world.

You can see wild mallards – the males have shiny green heads – on ponds, lakes and rivers everywhere. In many places, humans introduced them there.

It's harder to keep ducks than chickens because they need water. In Europe, ducks became food for rich people. But in parts of Asia, where rice is grown in watery plots called **paddy fields**, they have kept ducks alongside their rice for centuries.

Ducks are called ducks because they duck their heads **underwater**. Dabbling ducks keep their bottoms out of water, but diving ducks go right under.

Mallards (and domestic ducks) use their beaks as **sieves**. They take a mouthful from the pond, push the water out with their tongues and eat what's left.

Ducks don't freeze in cold water because their outside feathers are waterproof and their inside feathers (known as **down**) are warm. People use down for bedding and clothes.

Not all ducks **quack**. The only duck that makes a quacking sound is the female mallard. The male makes a different rasping sound.

Humans find ducks funny because of their **waddling** walk. Donald Duck is the most famous comic duck.

47 KANGAROO

Australia is far away from any other country. That's why many of its mammals can be found nowhere else. Many of them are **marsupials**, including the koala, wombat and the kangaroo.

Most mammals – humans included – spend a long time growing inside our mothers before we are born. But marsupials are born after a very short period inside. After being born, they clamber into a **pouch** on their mother's body. A kangaroo mother gives birth after 33 days and then her baby spends the next eight months in her pouch. Humans do a lot more growing inside our mothers than marsupials.

There are four kinds of kangaroo. The biggest, the **red kangaroo**, can grow to two metres tall. Kangaroos are **herbivores**, which means they feed on plant material.

Kangaroos travel by jumping and they are more **efficient** at moving than any other mammal on Earth. Red kangaroos cruise at around 25 km/h, with a top speed of 70 km/h.

When the first kangaroo came to London in 1791, it was a sensation. People thought it was **primitive** – not as good as the animals you find elsewhere – but this is certainly not the case.

The kangaroo is the official animal of Australia. Many Australians are proud of this and wave inflatable kangaroos to support their country at **cricket** matches.

40,000 years ago there was an Australian marsupial that was like a big cat. It was called the marsupial lion. And less than 100 years ago there was a marsupial that was like a dog or a wolf. This was the **thylacine**.

We know very little about the life of wild thylacines. No one knows how they **hunted**. Perhaps they were chasers? Perhaps they lay in wait and pounced? Perhaps they hunted in groups? It's most likely that they hunted mostly at night, and smelled out kangaroos and wallabies. And no one knows how they **lived**: whether they lived in packs like wolves or on their own.

Many thylacines were shot to stop them eating sheep. They also got distemper, a disease they caught from pet dogs. Their natural habitats were also destroyed, as much of the land they hunted on became farmland.

In 1886 the Tasmanian government paid **£1** (the equivalent of £128 today) for every dead thylacine. They saw them only as problem animals that killed their sheep.

There have been attempts to see if there are still wild thylacines out there, but an **expedition** in 1972 found nothing. However, every year there are people who think they have seen a thylacine in the Australian bush.

The thylacine is also known as the **Tasmanian tiger**.

The thylacine is still considered an important animal in Tasmania. It appears on the country's **coat of arms** and on their vehicle licence plates.

The last thylacine died in **Hobart Zoo**, Tasmania, in 1936. He looked like a big, stripy and rather unhappy dog. His name was Benjamin.

49 CROCODILE

Crocodiles live in the water, but they don't just eat fish. The big ones sometimes leap out of the water to eat large mammals.

But there's something about crocodiles that **scares** us. You've probably seen pictures of crocodiles grabbing wildebeest when they try to cross the river.

When the wildebeest have all crossed the river and moved on, the crocodiles probably won't eat a proper meal for another year. They can hold on for so long without eating because they're not mammals. They're **reptiles**.

We mammals heat our blood ourselves, and to do that we need a lot of food to supply the power. But crocodiles let the sun warm their blood, so they don't need so much fuel.

There are 14 species of crocodile, but only 2 species will eat humans: the **Nile crocodile** of Africa and the **saltwater crocodile** of Asia and northern Australia.

Crocodiles are ancient. They lived alongside the dinosaurs but, unlike them, they weren't wiped out by the meteor that hit Earth **65 million** years ago.

Crocodiles have the strongest bite in the world. Their bite is nearly **40 times** stronger than ours, and more than **7 times** stronger than a lion's. They have a flap in their mouths that closes up tight, so they can bite underwater without drowning.

Female crocodiles are **tender** and **gentle** mothers. They often hold their babies in their mouths to protect them.

We have made crocodiles the villains in many stories, like *Peter Pan* by J. M. Barrie and *The Elephant's Child* by Rudyard Kipling.

50 HORSE

Humans first caught horses for food. But once we started to **ride** them and use them to pull carts, humans were able to do things that had never been possible before. It was as if we had been given superpowers.

We began to keep horses for transport about 6,000 years ago in Central Asia. The first person who jumped on a horse's back probably fell off a moment later, but it was the beginning of a new way of life.

Humans could now travel long distances. A healthy horse can travel 160 kilometres a day at about 13 km/h, **twice** the speed and almost **four times** the distance a human can manage. A human can carry 20 kilograms: a horse can carry more than 90 kilograms.

Once we had horses, humans could **travel**. We could trade goods. We could visit each other. We could go to war. Our cities were full of horses. Horses even pulled **buses**. The human world was powered by horses. (Until we invented the engine.)

Horses have very big eyes set high on their heads so that they can see all about them while grazing with their heads down.

Horses run on their **hooves**. It's as if they run on a single toenail. It's one of the secrets of their speed.

Horses were used for farming: to pull ploughs and carts, and for rounding up cattle.

Since the invention of the engine, we rarely use horses for **transport**, to plough our fields or to carry heavy loads, but we still love horses and we now use them for fun. Many people ride just because they love to be around horses.

We think of horses as pretty special animals. There are many famous **paintings** of great horses, often ridden by kings and emperors.

Everything changed with the invention of the **stirrup**. This was more difficult than it sounds: to use stirrups you need a special saddle that doesn't hurt a horse: a horse in pain can't work properly. It's much easier to stay on a horse when you've got stirrups.

People were then able to ride horses into battle: a **mounted solider** was faster and more dangerous than one in a chariot. Warriors on horseback were important people. They were called knights. The cavalry, with many soldiers on many horses, became a powerful weapon.

Horses live in herds and they communicate with each other using body language, sound and touch.

51 OWL

Through the darkness, you hear a strange and **eerie** call. It makes you feel a little afraid. It's an owl. The human fear of the dark is summed up by the voice of an owl: the bird that loves the **night**.

We humans are daylight creatures and always have been. For us, light is safety and comfort. But the owl is a creature of the night and is awake during the darkness.

Throughout history the owl stands for our fear of all the evil things that might come out of the darkness.

There are about 200 species of owl. The smallest is the **elf owl**, which is 13.5 centimetres long, and the biggest is a female **Eurasian eagle owl** (female owls are mostly bigger), which can be 71 centimetres long.

Owls have brilliant **hearing**, and they can fly without making a sound. They don't make a noise that might interfere with their own pinpoint hearing.

It's hard to find your friends – or your enemies – in the dark. So when owls want to reach out to each other, they call. For an owl it simply means, 'I'm here – where are you?'

Owls are found on every continent apart from **Antarctica**.

52 SEAL

Humans have hunted seals for centuries: for their meat, fur, leather that can be made from their skins and the oil that can be made from their bodies, which was used for lamps.

But in the 1960s newspapers showed images of humans killing and harming harp seal cubs. Many people were **horrified**. They found this to be cruel and unnecessary and wanted to put a stop to it. They realised that we need to look after the **planet** and its creatures. Many countries now have laws against the trade in dead seals.

There are more than 30 species of seals. These include sea lions and walruses. The smallest is the **Baikal seal**, which weighs about 45 kilograms, and the largest is the **southern elephant seal**, which can weigh up to 3,200 kilograms.

Seals have collapsible lungs and insulating layers of **blubber** and fur to help them when they take long, deep dives to hunt for food.

Although the trade in seals has decreased, many species still face problems, such as the **melting** polar ice.

53 BOWERBIRD

If you make something beautiful on purpose and to please others – like the *Mona Lisa* by Leonardo da Vinci or Vincent van Gogh's *Sunflowers* – are you making art?

If so, male bowerbirds are **artists**. They make structures from twigs and decorate them with immense care: not for themselves but to attract female bowerbirds.

For decoration they use feathers, shells, leaves, flowers, stones, berries, bits of glass, plastic, coins and nails. One bird was even spotted using a **toy soldier**, another a plastic elephant.

The females choose the bower they like best, and pair up with the male that made it.

There are **20 species** of bowerbird. They all live in Australia and New Guinea. They can be found in different habitats, such as rainforest, eucalyptus woodland, acacia and scrub.

Different species have favourite colours. **Satin bowerbirds** like blue to match the colour of their feathers.

People have deliberately **messed up** bowers. When they've gone the bowerbird comes back and makes everything exactly as it was before.

Bowerbirds, like many species of bird, can see **ultraviolet** light, so they hunt for objects that reflect this light, like plastic bottle tops.

54 ELEPHANT

If you meet an elephant when you're out on a walk, you either wait for the elephant to pass or go another way. You must show an elephant respect. That's what the **first humans** did when they walked the African plains.

That became harder when humans started to become farmers. You can't move a farm out of an elephant's way. Elephants began to raid crops and they still do.

But humans have always loved elephants. They have played a big part in the cultures and religions of many countries.

Cynthia Moss, a **conservationist**, has spent most of her life with African elephants. She discovered that elephants bury dead members of their herd. Before that people thought only humans understood death. Cynthia showed us that elephants are very **complicated** animals with deep family ties.

Elephants are the largest living land animal. They are so big they can't jump or run. They must always be in contact with the earth. An African male elephant can stand **3.9 metres** tall at the shoulder and weigh 6,000 kilograms.

In 1930 there were around 10 million elephants in Africa, but today there are only 415,000.

There are three species of elephant: the **Asian elephant**, the **African bush elephant** and the **African forest elephant**.

AFRICAN FOREST ELEPHANT

AFRICAN BUSH ELEPHANT

ASIAN ELEPHANT

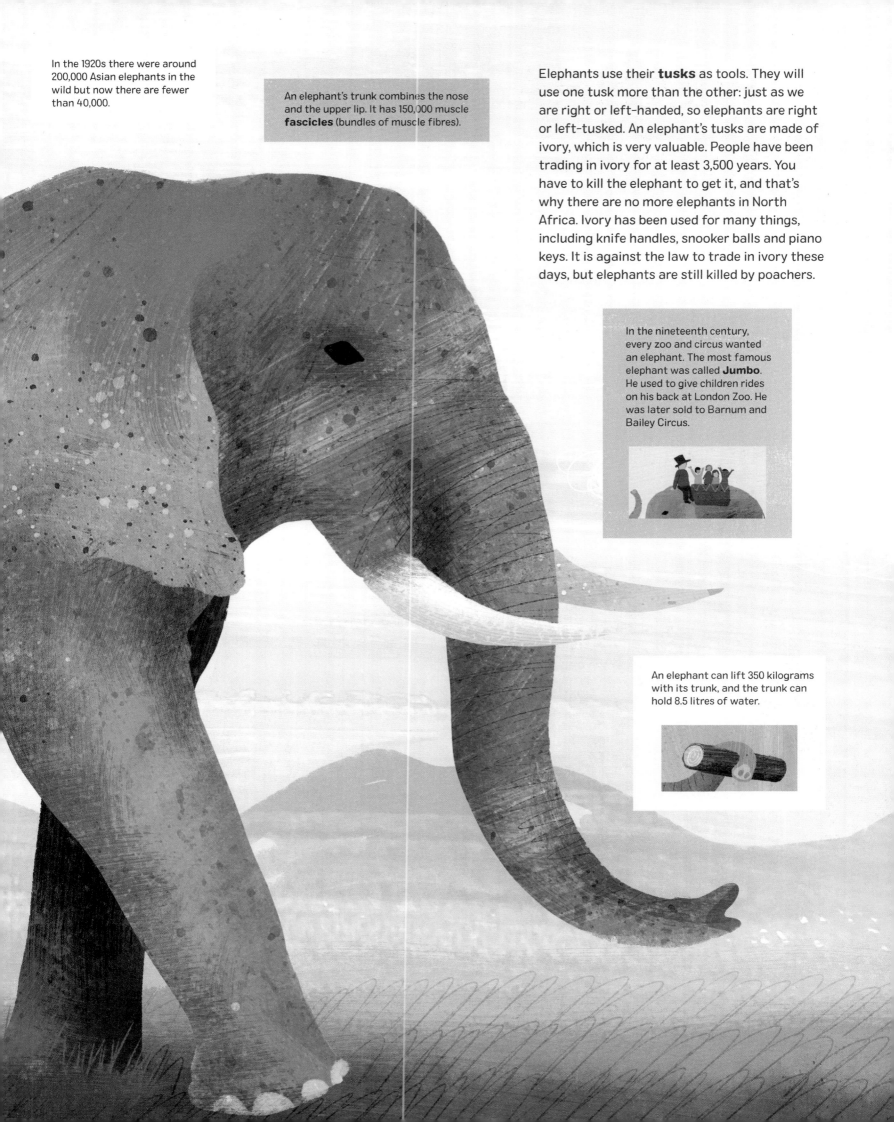

In the 1920s there were around 200,000 Asian elephants in the wild but now there are fewer than 40,000.

An elephant's trunk combines the nose and the upper lip. It has 150,000 muscle **fascicles** (bundles of muscle fibres).

Elephants use their **tusks** as tools. They will use one tusk more than the other: just as we are right or left-handed, so elephants are right or left-tusked. An elephant's tusks are made of ivory, which is very valuable. People have been trading in ivory for at least 3,500 years. You have to kill the elephant to get it, and that's why there are no more elephants in North Africa. Ivory has been used for many things, including knife handles, snooker balls and piano keys. It is against the law to trade in ivory these days, but elephants are still killed by poachers.

In the nineteenth century, every zoo and circus wanted an elephant. The most famous elephant was called **Jumbo**. He used to give children rides on his back at London Zoo. He was later sold to Barnum and Bailey Circus.

An elephant can lift 350 kilograms with its trunk, and the trunk can hold 8.5 litres of water.

PIRANHA

You have probably heard stories about piranhas, about how they live in great **shoals** and eat anything or anyone that dares to step into the water.

But it doesn't really happen like that. In one lake in **Brazil**, there were 190 piranha attacks on people in six months – all bitten toes. There have been human deaths from piranhas, but they're very unusual.

The piranha legend began when Theodore Roosevelt – the US president who gave his name to the teddy bear – was travelling in Brazil. The local people wanted to **impress** him, so they netted off a section of the river and filled it with piranhas before he got there.

When Roosevelt arrived, the place was heaving with very hungry and horribly stressed piranhas, and when they drove a poor old cow into the water, the cow was indeed eaten.

Roosevelt thought this happened all the time, so he wrote about it and created a **legend**.

There are about **60 species** of piranhas. They live in lakes and rivers in South America and gather together, not to hunt but to avoid being eaten themselves.

People who live by these rivers have used piranha **teeth** for carving wood, cutting hair and sharpening darts for blowpipes.

Piranha teeth are seriously sharp. They will bite a chunk from something bigger than themselves and then swim away.

Piranhas mostly eat fish. They also eat fruit, seeds and leaves that fall into the river.

TIT/CHICKADEE

It seems like we think that nature is waging war on us humans, and that we must do everything we can to fight back. But we can't keep it up. Again and again, we go out of our way to help wild creatures for no other reason than our own pleasure.

So we **feed** the birds. We not only put out kitchen scraps, we buy special food and leave it outside in special containers to make the birds happy. The birds that appreciate this most are the tits and chickadees.

They hang upside down from these feeders, eating **seeds**, peanuts and fat balls, and we watch them and feel better about ourselves and our place in the world.

Tits and chickadees are in the family called **Paridae**. You can find them all across the northern hemisphere and down to the bottom of Africa.

Tits and chickadees are natural **problem-solvers**. They have been known to open milk bottles left on doorsteps to feed on the cream that rises to the top.

The great scientist Edward O. Wilson said that humans naturally reach out for non-human life. He called this kind of love **biophilia**.

Half the adults in the UK and a third of the adults in the USA feed birds. In the USA people spend over **$3 billion** every year on bird food.

57 SPIDER

Many people are **frightened** of spiders, even though very few spiders can do us harm. In fact, they make some people feel uncomfortable just by the way they move.

You know that this fear is silly. You know that the spider before you – in the bath, scuttling across the bedroom floor – is likely to be **harmless**. And yet some of us still feel scared.

This probably comes from the strange way spiders move on their eight legs, which is completely different to the way humans and other mammals move. But spiders are wonderful. If you suffer from a fear of spiders (which is known as **arachnophobia**), you must try to think of their wonder as well.

Spiders make seven different kinds of **silk**. It comes out of their bodies. **Trapdoor spiders** make a silk-lined tunnel. **Water spiders** make a silken diving bell so they can live underwater.

Spiders don't just make webs with their silk. They also use it for catching **prey**, making shelters, as food, for nests, for safety lines to catch them should they fall and to tell them when enemies are coming.

Spiders even use silk to fly. They make a long line that catches the wind and blows them into the air. Sometimes they travel enormous distances this way.

If a spider gets stuck in your bath, you can leave it a ladder of toilet paper, so that it can climb back out again and return to its home.

Some of the largest spiders are **tarantulas**. They can have a leg span of up to 25 centimetres.

There are 50,000 species of spider. Most of them can't possibly hurt a human, and only a few species can kill people. There were around **100** reported deaths from spider bites in the whole of the twentieth century.

SILKWORM

Many creatures make silk. Some moths and butterflies wrap themselves up in silk as they grow. Before a caterpillar can turn into an adult with wings it must become a **pupa**. That's an in-between stage: it's as if the creature goes to bed a caterpillar and wakes up as a moth. Before a silk moth caterpillar becomes a pupa it wraps itself up with silk.

5,000 years ago, Chinese people learned how to use this silk to make **clothes**, and that is the silk that we wear. It comes from a silkworm: the caterpillar that spins a silky overcoat before it becomes a pupa.

To use the silk for humans, you must first boil the cocoon and kill the pupa. It takes between 2,000–3,000 cocoons to make just **450 grams** of silk.

Silkworms are domestic animals, like cows and pigs, and they are kept on silk farms. They couldn't survive in the wild: the adults can't even fly.

Silk makes strong, light, comfortable clothes. You can dye it many colours. Silk clothes are cool in summer and warm in winter.

The Chinese kept silkworms a **secret** for centuries. They didn't want anyone else to make silk. There is a story that a princess smuggled silkworms out of China by hiding them in her hair.

Silk became an important trade between Asia and Europe. The route for carrying the silk became known as the **Silk Road**. It was first used 2,000 years ago.

You can get 900 metres of thread from a single cocoon.

Silk was an important business in Europe. Silk cloth was made on big machines called **looms**. These looms knew what kind of cloth to make because they got their instructions – their programmes – from a system of punched cards. The loom was the first computer.

59 FALCON

Once humans had learned to grow their own plants instead of looking for them, and how to keep domestic animals instead of hunting them, it was possible – at least for rich people – to look for **entertainment**.

And so they went hunting. But now they hunted for fun not need. The best fun came from hunting birds with a tame falcon.

Falcons are **thrilling** birds to watch: the best and fastest fliers. To let your own falcon – a bird you carry on your gloved fist – fly after a bird was the next best thing to being a falcon yourself.

The better your bird, the more important you were. Flying a top falcon was like driving a Ferrari: perhaps even better, because it's more beautiful. A man flying a bird not only looked like a great lord, he truly felt like one.

There are 40 species of falcon, but other birds of prey can also be trained for falconry. Today the **Harris's hawk** is the most popular. They have been called 'the Labradors of falconry', as they are social and cooperative with humans.

The **peregrine falcon** is reckoned to be the best: fast, dramatic and able to kill birds much bigger than itself. It can reach up to 320 km/h in a dive.

People have been flying falcons for 4,000 years. It's said that **falconry** was the favourite sport of every king of England from Alfred the Great to George III. That's about 1,000 years' worth of kings.

Training a falcon is hard work and very difficult. Falconry fell out of fashion when it was possible to kill birds for fun with a shotgun.

60 PHEASANT

The **Romans** brought pheasants to Europe 2,000 years ago because they look handsome and because they could be eaten. But hundreds of years later, humans invented the shotgun. Now it was easy to kill birds for fun.

A shotgun fires a handful of lead pellets instead of a single bullet, which makes it easier to kill a flying bird.

It became obvious that pheasants were the perfect **target**. They are big and fly slowly. It is, then, quite easy to shoot them with a shotgun. In many places, pheasants were brought in, fed and looked after, just so that rich people could have the fun of shooting them.

In Britain, **40 million** pheasants are turned loose into the countryside every year.

There are 50 species in the pheasant family (known as **Phasianidae**). They eat seeds, insects and small mammals and reptiles.

In the ninteenth century, any creature that might harm a pheasant was killed, if at all possible. That included falcons and other **birds of prey**. Five species were wiped out in the UK: the marsh harrier, osprey, white-tailed eagle, honey buzzard and goshawk.

In 1903 King George V shot 1,000 pheasants in six days in a **competition** with a friend. His friend still won.

In 1954 a law was passed in the UK to stop people shooting birds of prey. But many birds of prey continue to be shot.

61 BARNACLE

Barnacles stick. It's what they're best at. They stick to rocks on the **seashore**, they stick to piers and they stick to the bottom of ships.

This can slow a ship down by 40 per cent. It's like driving a car with the handbrake on. The US Navy spends an estimated **$500 million** a year getting barnacles off ships.

People have been trying to get rid of barnacles for years, but barnacles are difficult to shift.

Barnacles are related to crabs and insects. They are part of an enormous group, with over a million species, called **arthropods**.

Charles Darwin spent eight years studying barnacles. He did it to establish his reputation as a **scientist** – so that people would take his theory of evolution seriously.

Once when Darwin's children visited friends, one of them was puzzled and asked, 'But where does your daddy keep his barnacles?'

62 HEAD LOUSE

You're brilliant, you're beautiful and altogether wonderful, but for a head louse you're just a **meal** and a nice place to live.

Head lice cling to human hairs and feed on blood. They are annoying but mostly harmless: though you can get an infection if you scratch the bites too much.

In the UK, two thirds of primary-school pupils have head lice at some stage.

The easiest way to get rid of head lice is to shave all your hair off. That's why 300 years ago all the people who could afford to wore **wigs**. Today we can get rid of lice by using a very fine-tooth comb or special shampoo.

Other animals that can make their homes on (or in) humans include **body lice**, **Demodex mites** that live in your eyelashes and **intestinal worms** that live in your gut and can be up to 30 metres long.

Head lice can be up to 3 millimetres long and they don't have wings. They spend their entire lives on a human head.

63 CROW

We like and admire most intelligent animals: elephants, dolphins, chimpanzees. Crows are as **clever** as any of these, but they have often been hated.

They were thought to be birds that bring **bad luck**: if your best cow died, you would probably find a crow feeding on its body. They were sometimes shot on sight, as enemies to humans. In historic battles, they were known to feed on the bodies of fallen soliders.

They are smart and can eat almost anything: so they are good at feeding on the food that humans leave lying around. Crows took corn from humans as soon as humans started farming. Today crows will even eat chips.

Crows are mostly harmless to us humans. But many people still dislike them.

There are 120 species of corvid, including **crows**, **rooks**, **jays** and **magpies**. Not all of them are black.

In Japan, crows put nuts on roads so that passing cars will crack them open. They improved this method by putting the nuts on a pedestrian crossing and collecting the nuts when it's safe.

New Caledonian crows make and use **tools**, such as hooks to reach insects.

When a crow finds a dead mammal, the first thing it eats are the eyes. That's the easiest bit to get at, but it's a habit that humans find upsetting.

Some people think it's the crows' fault that we have fewer **songbirds** in the world these days. Scientists have proved them wrong, but many people still believe this.

Crows have an excellent **memory**.

BAT

Humans have always been troubled by the night: and bats, like owls, can remind us of our fear of the **dark**.

We have made up stories about bat-like humans because of this fear: the vampire **Count Dracula**, who sucks the blood of humans in the night, and the superhero **Batman**.

Bats are mammals like us, but they are the only mammals that can fly. Most smaller bats find their way in the dark by sound. Their sound-picture of the world is a bit like the human invention **radar**. Bats beat humans to the discovery by several million years.

Most small bats eat insects, but **vampire bats** are small, with a wingspan of about 18 centimetres, and they drink blood. They land on the ground and crawl to reach larger mammals. When they have found one, they bite and drink. They will drink the blood of humans if they get a chance.

There are approximately 1,300 species of bats. **One-fifth** of all mammal species are bats.

A lot of animals can glide. But only four groups have learned how to **fly** under their own power by flapping: birds, insects, bats and the extinct pterosaurs (which include pterodactyls).

The biggest bats have a wingspan of two metres, like the **giant golden-crowned flying fox**, and the smallest, the **bumblebee bat**, has a wingspan of less than 15 centimetres.

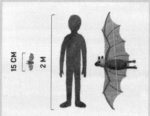

For the Chinese bats are lucky. The word *fu* in Mandarin means 'bat', and it also means good luck.

Count Dracula first appeared in 1897 in a book of the same name by Bram Stoker. It's clear that **Dracula** is a horribly sinister character when he is seen climbing down his castle wall – his head pointing downwards.

65 BUMBLEBEE

How do flowering plants make more flowering plants? It begins when **pollen** is moved from a flower on one plant to a flower on another.

Many plants get insects like bumblebees to do this job. The flowers offer the bees a sweet liquid called **nectar**; the bees drink it and accidentally pick up pollen as they do so. Then they move on to another flower.

This is a life-and-death matter for us humans, because a lot of what we eat comes from flowering plants. Every piece of fruit or vegetable we eat we owe to insects.

There are fewer insects around to do the job these days because of all the chemicals we use. In some places farmers even have to pay people to bring in **domestic honeybees**.

Bumblebees are mostly active in the warmer months of the year. They start work early in spring, protected by their furry coats.

Plants that need pollination include potatoes, onions, cabbages, sugar beets, oranges, lemons, coffee, coconuts, apples, mangoes, peas, broccoli, strawberries, aubergines, tomatoes . . . I've hardly begun but I haven't got room for anymore.

A study suggested that without insects a **third** of the world's crops would die in the fields.

POLLEN

Bumblebees are just one of many **wild animals** that carry pollen. Others include wasps, flies, butterflies, moths, beetles, midges, mosquitoes, bats, birds, monkeys, rodents and even some lizards.

Some people think scientists can't explain how a bumblebee can fly. In fact, they can – a bumblebee flies more like a helicopter than a fixed wing aircraft.

66 SALMON

Salmon thrill humans. They leap up waterfalls. They **travel** for hundreds of kilometres to get back home. Some people find them exciting to catch with a fishing rod. Many find them delicious to eat.

Salmon leave the rivers where they hatched and swim out to sea. Years later, they come back to the rivers to mate and lay eggs.

For most of the fish, this means that their lives are complete and they will die. Bears and eagles come from the **forests** to feast on them. Salmon are food from the sea – and the forest thrives on it.

People pay big money to fish for salmon. Catching a salmon is a great pleasure to some people.

There are nine species of salmon that people eat. The **Atlantic salmon** and then eight species of **Pacific salmon**.

The **chinook** and **sockeye salmon** of Idaho, USA, swim 1,400 kilometres from the Pacific Ocean and climb around 2,100 metres to return home.

Wild salmon are hatched in rivers. They swim down to the sea, where they spend most of their lives. Most fish can only live in fresh water or seawater. But salmon can do both.

There aren't enough wild fish left to feed all the world's humans. In the last 100 years we have started to farm fish – especially salmon. But there are problems with farming fish. Waste food and the **chemicals** used to keep the fish healthy all get into the sea.

A salmon from a **fish farm** has spent most of its life crammed together with other fish, as tight as humans on a busy train, sometimes swimming in its own poo. A large amount of Atlantic salmon is now farmed in this way.

ORYX

We love unicorns. They crop up in stories, books and films, and as pictures and toys. They are magical creatures that never existed, but they matter to us – and it's likely we got the idea from the oryx.

We have had **unicorns** in our lives for a good 3,000 years: sometimes believing they were real, sometimes just loving the idea of them.

Oryxes are horse-like antelopes. See one sideways and it seems to have a single horn: for a moment you think you could be looking at a unicorn.

It was said that unicorns could make **poisonous** water drinkable, and that their horns could cure all kinds of illness. Christians believed unicorns were so pure that they were linked with the Virgin Mary.

Oryxes are dry-country antelopes that can live without water for a long time. There are four species: the **scimitar-horned oryx**, the **Arabian oryx**, the **East African oryx** and the **South African oryx**.

The scimitar-horned oryx became **extinct** in the wild in 2000, but there are a few thousand left in captivity. Some of these have been released to form half-wild protected herds.

The Arabian oryx was hunted too much and became extinct in the wild. But a few were left in zoos. These were brought together in Phoenix, USA, and a **new herd** was built up. Arabian oryxes have been released back into the wild and are doing well.

Unicorns feature in many stories, such as *Alice Through the Looking-Glass* by Lewis Carroll, Walt Disney's film *Fantasia* and in *The Chronicles of Narnia* by C. S. Lewis. Every magical story is better for having a unicorn in it.

Oryxes are herbivores, which means they eat grass and plants. They are able to go without water for long periods of time.

68 SHEEP

Sheep were one of the first large mammals that humans kept for food. There have been domestic sheep for about 13,000 years.

That's because sheep are **easy**. They're not as fierce as cattle and pigs. And they stick together in a **flock**: so one human can control a lot of them. A person that looks after sheep is called a shepherd.

Sheep can also live on less food than bigger animals, and they can live on quite poor pasture.

In fact, sheep are useful to humans in many ways. You can milk sheep and drink the **milk** or make **cheese** from it. You can use their wool for clothes and bedding, and you can eat their meat.

Sheep were very imporant and that's why sheep come into so many **religions**. In Christianity, Jesus is called the good shepherd, and those who turn to him are often called his flock. And Muhammad, the founder of the Islamic religion, said, 'There was no prophet who was not a shepherd.'

Sheep have always played a big part in daily life. That's why they appear in many nursery rhymes, such as 'Mary had a Little Lamb', and 'Little Bo Peep has lost her Sheep'.

People bred fierce dogs to protect their sheep from wolves and other humans – dogs such as the **German shepherd**.

In 1996 scientists managed to make a sheep by copying it – almost like a printer on a computer – from another sheep. The process is called **cloning** and the sheep was called Dolly.

69 NENE (OR HAWAIIAN GOOSE)

Ever since humans became farmers we have been fighting **nature**. It always seemed as if nature was enormous and humans were tiny – an underdog species in a difficult and dangerous world. But it's now the other way round – humans are damaging nature.

In 1950 Peter Scott saw that the nene was about to become **extinct**, and he decided to do something about it. It was the start of a new understanding of the world; humans now had to look after nature.

The nene is a goose that lives only on the islands of **Hawaii**, and there were only 32 of them left before Scott started to raise nenes in the UK and return them to Hawaii.

It is clear that if we humans want nature, we have to work very hard to protect it.

Nenes are geese that don't like water. They live on the Hawaiian **lava plains** – landscapes made by volcanoes – and don't even have fully webbed feet.

The nenes didn't bounce back at once. There were problems with **mongooses**, which ate the eggs and chicks. People had taken mongooses to Hawaii to get rid of rats and snakes, but they did that and then started eating nene eggs. So people had to get rid of the mongoose – not easy!

There are now about **2,500** nenes on the islands of Hawaii. Many other Hawaiian birds have become extinct. We got to the nene just in time.

Peter Scott set up the Severn Wildfowl Trust in 1946 – one of the first organisations to protect nature. It is now the **Wildfowl and Wetlands Trust.**

70 ORANG-UTAN

Orang-utans are great **apes**, along with chimpanzees and gorillas – and humans. They live in hot, wet forests in Asia. They are good climbers and spend most of their time in trees.

They are smart, as you would expect. They use and make tools. Every night they make a shelter in the **treetops** to keep warm and dry.

As Charles Darwin worked on his big idea – the idea that humans and all other animals are related – he was fascinated by an orang-utan in London Zoo. Her name was Jenny. She was dressed in clothes and trained to drink tea: her links with us **humans** were obvious to all. Darwin said that Jenny was 'like a child' and praised her intelligence.

Orang-utans don't spend as much time in company as the other great apes. That's why their faces aren't as lively and expressive as chimpanzees.

Orang-utan means '**person of the forest**' in Malay. They only live on the islands of Borneo and Sumatra. There are three species: **Bornean**, **Sumatran** and **Tapanuli orang-utan**.

TAPANULI
SUMATRAN
BORNEAN

The adult male orang-utans live mostly **alone**. But the females spend up to five years with a youngster and teach him or her how to live in the forest. It's like going to school.

Rainforests have been around for a long time, so orang-utans have had millions of years to specialise in living there. They have specialised brilliantly, but that means they can't live anywhere else. If we destroy the forests, we will destroy the orang-utans.

In Sumatra and Borneo, where orang-utans live, forests are being chopped down to grow oil palms. We use palm oil in all kinds of things, such as bread, crisps, margarine, soap, shampoo, ice cream, pizza, instant noodles, chocolate, detergent, lipstick, biscuits . . .

On average a person uses eight kilograms of palm oil a year. This means that more and more forests get cut down. So when we shop, we need to be careful what we buy, and make sure that any palm oil comes from a good place.

The rainforests are important for orang-utans, but they are important for everything else that lives there too. These forests are jumping with life of all kinds. They are also important for everything else that lives on the planet. They help keep the Earth cool and suitable for life. They are like a great air-conditioning plant.

We can only save the orang-utans by saving their forests.

All three orang-utan species are classified as **Critically Endangered**. There are only about 800 Tapanuli orang-utans left in the wild.

71 PARROT

We have always liked parrots. They make us laugh. They are as bright and **colourful** as clowns, and they remind us of ourselves.

They sit upright on a perch, like a human on a chair. They use a foot like a hand to eat a nut as we do an ice-cream cornet. And, above all, some species can talk. They use human words and human voices.

They are as **clever** as non-human great apes, dolphins and crows. Parrots have been trained to use words with their proper meanings.

But they make rotten pets. In the wild, most parrots live closely with a partner, so a parrot kept on its own focuses on its owner. If they are left alone, they can become very lonely and unhappy, sometimes even plucking out their feathers.

Yet many parrots have been taken from the wild to become pets. The **Spix's macaw** was such a popular pet that it is now extinct in the wild.

There are more than 350 species of parrot. The biggest, the **hyacinth macaw**, is a metre long (from head to the tip of its tail) and the smallest, the **buff-tailed pygmy parrot**, is only 8 centimetres.

A hyacinth macaw has a **bite** as powerful as a big dog.

A pet parrot called N'Kisi knew **1,000** different words and it's been claimed he used them properly, knowing exactly what they meant.

Parrots feature in many stories. Long John Silver, the pirate in *Treasure Island* by Robert Louis Stevenson always had a parrot perched on his shoulder.

Pet parrots have gone wild in many cities of the world, including London, where you can often see **ring-necked parakeets**.

72 COLORADO BEETLE

An adult beetle can eat around 10 square centimetres of leaf in a day.

Colorado beetles eat plants like buffalo bur and nightshade. They can eat any relative of these plants.

These relatives include potatoes, aubergines and tomatoes. By planting these crops humans accidentally created a perfect world for Colorado beetles.

Humans fought back, creating many different **chemicals** designed to kill the beetles. But these have often damaged much more than just the beetles.

When Americans sold potatoes to Europe, the beetles came with them.

Not all beetles were killed by the chemicals. They lived and had young that also survived. Most of the Colorado beetles today are untroubled by the chemicals we use now.

Colorado beetles have been wiped out in the UK at least **163** times.

73 LOCUST

Locusts have been a problem for humans ever since we started to farm.

Most of the time locusts live like ordinary grasshoppers, causing no trouble to anyone. But when they get **overcrowded** they change.

They eat more, they breed more and they fly together. They form **swarms** of billions of insects. Each locust can eat its own weight in plants in a day.

When locusts behave like this, it is called a **plague**. These plagues can ruin crops that humans plant.

Between 1966 and 1969, a plague of locusts travelled all over Africa. In 2013 another plague covered half of Madagascar.

Once a locust plague has begun it is very hard to stop. It is best to get to the swarm before the numbers have started to build up, and kill them.

74 BAIJI (OR CHINESE RIVER DOLPHIN)

Extinction is not something that happened once or which might happen in the future. It's happening right now.

In 2006 the baiji (or Chinese river dolphin) was declared **functionally extinct**, which means that the odd one or two might still turn up, but there is no chance of them recovering.

Baijis lived in the silt and murk of the great river system of **China**. Like bats, they found their way around by sound. They lived in a stretch of the Yangtze river that is 1,700 kilometres long.

The baijis had many problems in the Yangtze, which is the busiest river in the world. They were caught in fishing nets and **drowned**. They were hit by boats and injured by the propellers. People caught so many fish that the dolphins found it hard to catch their own.

There are different species of river dolphins still living in the **Ganges**, **Plate** and **Amazon** rivers.

A baiji could swim at 60 km/h in a hurry, and cruise at half that speed.

The boats in the Yangtze made such a noise that the dolphins found it almost impossible to make their sound pictures and find their way about.

Baijis were animals that loved to be together: very **intelligent** and good at communicating with each other.

2,000 years ago, there were 5,000 baijis. There were efforts to save them, but they came **too late**. Too much of the river had been changed by humans.

75 CRANE

Cranes have been called the birds of heaven. Some species stand nearly as **tall** as humans, they **dance** like ballerinas and they **fly** like angels. No wonder they are considered special birds all over the world.

In Japan, women from the Ainu people traditionally dress up as cranes and dance. **Valmiki**, a great Indian writer, invented India's greatest form of poetry after seeing a crane killed by an arrow. In Western Asia, the chief goddesses were called the **Three Cranes**.

In America, whooping cranes were becoming extinct fast; people shot them and their habitats were being destroyed. But after 1950 people began to try to save this incredible bird.

There are 15 species of crane. The **demoiselle crane** is 90 centimetres tall and the **sarus crane** can be 175 centimetres tall.

Male and female cranes mate for life. They dance together as a way of keeping together.

In Japan, there is a belief that if you make 1,000 paper cranes, a real crane will grant you a wish. Sadako Sasaki loved this idea and created her own flock of paper cranes before she died. She died of leukaemia, aged 12, as a result of the bomb that fell on **Hiroshima** in 1945. The paper crane is now a symbol of peace and hope.

Cranes became **extinct** in the UK 500 years ago, and came back of their own accord in the 1970s. Cranes have since been released in the UK. They are still pretty rare, though.

Cranes like to eat seeds, leaves, insects, worms and snails.

MAMMOTH

Mammoths were a great puzzle to people 250 years ago. People knew they existed from teeth, bones and tusks they had found in Siberia. So where were the living mammoths?

Some said they must have been wiped out. Others said they must still be alive somewhere. But a French scientist named **Georges Cuvier** dared to say that mammoths were extinct.

Cuvier said, quite reasonably, that if creatures as big as mammoths still existed, humans would surely have seen them. You couldn't miss a mammoth.

Cuvier was right. Humans had to accept that an entire species of animal could become **extinct**: never to be seen again. And there was a more difficult issue behind that – if mammoths could become extinct, then humans could as well.

Woolly mammoths lived in a wide ring round the **North Pole**, eating plants. They probably lived like modern elephants, in small groups led by a wise old female.

For humans who lived 10,000 years ago mammoths were food. **Shelters** could be made from their bones and their hairy hides.

The last mammoth lived only 4,000 years ago, on **Wrangel Island** in the Arctic. Mammoths shared the planet with modern humans. We only just missed them.

Mammoths are the best studied group of all extinct animals. We not only have their bones, but also their bodies and their droppings – which have been found buried in ice, as if kept for us in the deep freeze.

77 GOAT

Goats have been kept by humans for meat, milk and leather for thousands of years.

It's much harder to keep goats than sheep. Sheep eat grass, stick together and follow a leader. You can drive a flock of sheep wherever you want to. But goats eat trees and bushes. They climb enthusiastically – they will even **climb trees** – and they don't stay together in the same way. Put them in a field and a few of them will soon find a way out.

Goats can feed in **poor conditions**, where few other domestic animals could survive. After they have finished eating, it can be hard for the land to grow plants again.

All over the world deserts are getting bigger. The **Sahara Desert** extends 250 kilometres further south than it did in 1900. Goats are often the last animals to get any nutrients from these desert lands.

A goatskin can be used to carry liquids. It's a convenient size and it stretches to take in fluid. With a goatskin a human could travel further into dry places.

In 2011 there were around **924 million** goats in the world.

78 LOA LOA WORM

The loa loa worm is a **nematode** worm. 28,000 species of nematodes have been discovered; 16,000 are parasites. 80 per cent of all the animals on the planet are nematodes.

Sometimes nature seems bright and beautiful. At other times it seems truly **horrible**. Take the loa loa worm.

The loa loa worm is a **parasite**: that is to say, it lives on or in another animal. The loa loa worm lives inside humans.

The worms cause painful **swellings** all over the body and when they reach the eye, the human host can go blind.

The loa loa worm can live in no other way than in humans. There is no injection to prevent it.

Loa loa worm means **'worm worm worm'**.

For a loa loa worm an uninfected human is a beautiful opportunity to live and make more worms.

Loa loa worms are found in the rainforests of West and Central Africa.

79 PEAFOWL

The great naturalist Charles Darwin said, 'The sight of a feather in a peacock's tail . . . makes me sick.'

That's because he couldn't explain it. How could the enormous and beautiful **tail** of a peacock help it live longer and make more peacocks?

Darwin thought and thought – and in the end he found the answer. The more glorious a peacock's tail, the more **attractive** he is to females.

The male peacock with the best tail will find more females to pair up with and to have baby peacocks and peahens with.

There are three species of peafowl: **Indian** (or blue peafowl), the **South East Asian** (or green peafowl) and the **Congo peafowl**.

A female has no lovely tail; she is called a **peahen**.

Humans have always loved peacocks for their beauty, and often rich people keep them to admire. They're not expensive to keep but they need a lot of space.

Scientists have proven that humans find watching fish swim deeply **relaxing**.

But fish are hard to watch in a pond – unless they are a different colour to the water. In China 1,400 years ago, they kept Asian carp in ponds – and sometimes they produced a **golden oddity**.

The Chinese bred the golden fish for the pleasure of looking at them. Sometimes they caught them and put them in a porcelain bowl indoors. They were living treasures.

Later, the Japanese started to keep goldish and after that they were taken to Europe. Soon everybody loved them.

When glass became cheaper and easier to use in the nineteenth century, the **aquarium** was invented. Soon it became easier for ordinary people to keep fish at home.

Goldfish have **tetrachromatic** (four-colour) vision, which means they can see ultraviolet light.

Goldfish are intelligent; they can tell one human from another, and will beg from the person who feeds them. They have been trained to perform **tricks**.

Goldfish can remember things for at least **three** months. It's not true that they have poor memories.

Humans have bred goldfish into fancy forms that couldn't survive in the wild, such as **bubble eye**, **fantail**, **lionhead**, **pearlscale**, **pompom** and many others.

The idea that goldfish don't live very long is wrong. They die when they are badly looked after. A goldfish kept well can live for **15 years**.

81 CANARY

As soon as humans started living in cities we missed the things we had lost – trees, flowers and the sound of birds. Cities were full of human noise even before the invention of the motor car, and that just didn't sound right.

So people caught wild birds, put them in cages and listened to them **singing**. People did that all over the world, wherever there were cities.

People started keeping canaries in cages around 600 years ago. They were caught on islands off the coast of Africa, including the **Canary Islands**.

As soon as they reached Europe they were a huge success. They looked pretty, they sang beautifully and they were quite easy to keep.

Canary Islands means '**islands of dogs**'. So the pretty bird is named after a dog.

Caged birds were taken on sea voyages by sailors of many cultures, including Babylonians, Polynesians and Vikings.

In the seventeenth century, people started to take canaries down coal mines as **alarms**. Canaries are more sensitive to dangerous gas than humans, so when a canary got distressed, the miners knew it was time to get out fast. The last canary to go down a mine in the UK did so in **1986**.

Catching wild birds for their song has had a very **bad effect** on the wild bird population in some parts of Asia.

There aren't so many caged birds in Europe and the USA these days. We drown out the city noises with recorded **music** instead.

82 REINDEER

A sack full of presents, a white-bearded old man dressed in red and a sleigh pulled by reindeer: almost everyone in the world knows that means . . . **Christmas**.

But it's a fairly new idea all the same. The first story about Father Christmas and his reindeer was written in 1823. It appeared in a newspaper in New York, USA, and was called 'A Visit from St Nicholas'. It begins: "Twas the night before Christmas . . .'

Rudolph didn't appear for another century. Robert Lewis May wrote a poem about the **red-nosed** reindeer in 1939. Ten years later, his brother-in-law, Johnny Marks, set it to music. The song was recorded by Gene Autry, the Singing Cowboy, and sold 2.5 million copies in the first year. Now Father Christmas and his flying reindeer are known all over the world.

Wild reindeer are called **caribou** in the USA. They live in the coldest parts of the world all round the North Pole.

Reindeer can't fly, but they can do something even more brilliant: they can **survive** very cold weather – weather that would kill most other animals.

Reindeer are great travellers. Some herds travel 4,800 kilometres every year, more than any other land mammal.

Humans who live in cold places, such as **Alaska** and **Siberia**, have kept herds of reindeer for their meat and even used them to pull sleighs.

A reindeer's hooves are wide and crescent-shaped to help them walk across snow.

The world is getting **warmer**, which is causing problems for reindeer. They are brilliant at living in the cold, but they can't cope with heat.

83 TURKEY

We humans love a feast. We have been feasting since the first humans walked on the plains of Africa. When these early humans managed to kill a large animal, they had no choice but to **feast** – after all, meat goes off very quickly in a hot climate.

Ever since those times, we have celebrated special days by sitting down with friends and family to enjoy the best and biggest meal we can afford. In Europe and America, that usually means turkey. In the UK, people have turkeys for Christmas and in the USA they have them for the harvest festival called **Thanksgiving**.

Turkeys have been the centre of the feast for hundreds of years. And in the days after the feast, there is still plenty of food left.

Wild turkeys live in Central and North America. They were first domesticated at least 3,000 years ago.

The first turkey was brought to England in **1526** by the explorer William Strickland.

Turkeys were farmed in Norfolk and walked all the way to London before Christmas, around **240 kilometres**. That way they were fresh for the market. These days turkeys are usually frozen and sold in supermarkets.

At first turkeys were **expensive**. People more often had a goose or beef for Christmas. Now for many people Christmas is unthinkable without a turkey.

Turkeys are **omnivores** and they like to eat nuts, fruits, seeds and insects.

84 DEER

Once humans hunted deer in order to stay alive. Then they invented farming, and, with it, constant hard work. But much later, wealthy people began to hunt deer again, this time it was for fun.

Humans took to hunting deer all over the world, wherever you could find deer. This kind of hunting was for important people like **kings** and **nobles**.

When William the Conqueror left northern France and invaded England in 1066, he brought **hunting** with him. By the twelfth century one third of all southern England was a royal hunting estate.

Ordinary people were forbidden to keep dogs and own weapons. You could be hanged if you killed forest animals, as they belonged to the king.

Deer are found in every continent except Antarctica and Australia. Only one species lives in Africa, though.

The biggest deer is the **moose** (called elk in Europe). It is 2.6 metres at the shoulder. The smallest, the **northern pudú**, is 32 centimetres tall.

Around 20,000 years ago, people **painted** images of deer on cave walls. At Lascaux, France, around 90 deer paintings have been discovered.

Water deer don't have horns, but they have extra-long teeth for showing off and fighting.

The stories of **Robin Hood** are well known in the UK. They tell of a noble outlaw who lived in Sherwood Forest and hunted deer. He robbed the rich to give to the poor.

85 RABBIT

Rabbits are easy to keep. Put a wall round a grassy place, fill it with a few rabbits and soon you will have lots more rabbits. A female rabbit can have up to **60** young in a year.

Rabbits are very adaptable creatures. For centuries they have been caught and eaten by people, but as long as they have enough food they will keep reproducing.

The **Romans** probably brought rabbits to Britain, and so did the French after William the Conqueror in 1066. Since then, people have released rabbits on every continent except **Antarctica**.

But everywhere people took rabbits, the rabbits escaped and went wild. We have tried many different ways of getting rid of them. In the 1950s people introduced a disease called **myxomatosis**. It killed most of the rabbits – but their numbers have recovered since then.

People confuse rabbits and hares. Baby rabbits are **blind** and helpless little things born in a burrow. Baby hares are born in the open and can run straight away.

Bugs Bunny is a hare. So is Brer Rabbit in the old American stories. There were no wild rabbits in America until the late nineteenth century – only hares!

Rabbits produce two kinds of poo. One they put outside their burrow, and the other they eat. This is to get double the goodness out of their food.

Rabbits can produce a litter of between 4–12 babies (or **kits**).

There are many stories of clever rabbits beating their enemies by being **extra smart**. These stories remind us of the first humans, who lived on the African plains surrounded by big fierce animals. They too survived by being clever.

86 SPARROW

Long before humans became farmers, sparrows flew down to join us at **mealtimes** to feed on our scraps.

Then when we had farms and permanent homes, sparrows moved in with us: nesting in roofs and picking up anything we dropped in the way of food. Humans have always lived with the sound of **cheeping** sparrows.

When we moved into cities the sparrows came too. After all, we had horses, and horses need food – and any horse feed we spilled, the sparrows took for themselves.

But these days there are problems for sparrows. They can't find as much food in the **cities** as they once did, and the countryside is no longer an easy place for them.

There are two species of sparrows: **house sparrows** and **tree sparrows**. In Europe, we associate house sparrows with the city and tree sparrows with the countryside.

People tried to kill all the sparrows in China in the 1950s. But without the sparrows to eat them there were lots more locusts and other harmful insects.

There weren't any house sparrows in the USA – until a New Yorker called Eugene Schieffelin brought in a few in 1852.

If we want sparrows back in our **cities**, we need wilder gardens where sparrows can find food.

87 BUTTERFLY

Butterflies have been around for at least 200 million years. There are about **18,000** species.

Humans have always loved butterflies: it almost seems as if butterflies exist just to please our eyes with their **beauty**.

In the past some people believed that butterflies were the souls of humans that have passed away. In Japan, it's said that if a butterfly enters your house, the person you **love** best will soon be arriving.

The **peacock butterfly** frightens off birds that might eat it. The patterns on its wings look like the eyes of an owl.

Butterflies live in stages: first eggs, then caterpillars, **pupae** and finally fully grown butterflies.

Some butterflies are great travellers. **Painted lady butterflies** fly up from Africa as far as the Arctic Circle.

In the nineteenth century, people loved butterflies so much they caught and killed them in their hundreds, so they could admire their beauty at home.

88 FRUIT FLY

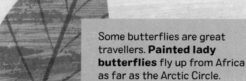

Scientists can now make different sorts of animals by playing with their genes. Some people think this will help humans in the future. Others think it could lead to disaster.

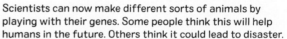
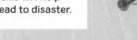

Your birth parents made you. My birth parents made me. You might look like your father, but also have your mother's eyes.

How does this work? Your parents pass on a mixture of their **genes** to you. Genes carry information that decides your traits, such as the colour of your hair or eyes.

So how do genes work? Since 1910 scientists have been studying the genes of the fruit fly. Fruit flies are good animals to study as they're easy to keep in **laboratories**. Because of the work on fruit flies, we are starting to understand how genes work.

At first scientists kept the fruit flies in **milk bottles** and fed them banana paste.

Fruit flies are easy animals to work with because you can clearly tell male from female. Males have black bottoms.

89 SAOLA

The saola is probably the last big land animal we humans will ever discover. 30 years ago hardly anyone on Earth knew it existed.

The reason for this was war. The saola is found only in **Vietnam** and **Laos**, but there had been war in that region for 50 years, which made it dangerous for scientists to explore.

When the war ended in 1973 people started to rebuild the country. A lot of forests had been destroyed in the war: some of what was left was made into the **Vū Quang National Park**.

Scientists explored these remaining forests and met a local hunter who had the skull of an unknown animal.

This animal turned out to be a **saola**, sometimes called the Vu Quang ox.

The saola looks like an antelope but it is more closely related to a cow. They can stand 84 centimetres at the shoulder and are 150 centimetres long.

Saolas are very hard to find, and harder still to watch. Even today no one knows very much about saolas. We have no idea how many of them are left in the world. One estimate says 750. No scientist has ever seen a wild one.

Saolas have sometimes been photographed on remote-controlled cameras.

During the Vietnam War a lot of forests were destroyed. The Americans dropped a chemical called **Agent Orange** to kill the trees. They did this because enemy soldiers often hid in the forest. Now some people in Vietnam are trying to replant the forests that were destroyed. The saola will only survive if we can help save the forests.

Saolas are found in the forests of the **Annamite Mountains** in Vietnam and Laos.

GIANT SQUID

Is it real? Or is it a fictional monster? Does the giant squid really live in the depths of the ocean? Or is it just a character in scary stories that we love to tell about the cruel sea?

Enormous squids and octopuses turn up in stories again and again. **Scylla** was a monster that was supposed to grab sailors from their boats with its tentacles.

The Scandinavians told tales about the **kraken**: a creature with many tentacles that lived in the seas off Norway and Greenland.

In all these stories the huge squids are as fierce as possible: dragging ships down with their tentacles and devouring sailors alive.

But some people tried to take a calmer view. Ancient thinkers like Aristotle and Pliny the Elder both wrote about a creature that sounded very like a giant squid.

Squids are **molluscs**: like octopuses they are related to snails and slugs.

The biggest giant squid found so far is **13 metres** long, with a body of 2 metres. The length is all in the tentacles.

13 METRES

Giant squids live in deep waters and hunt fish. They are eaten by **sperm whales**.

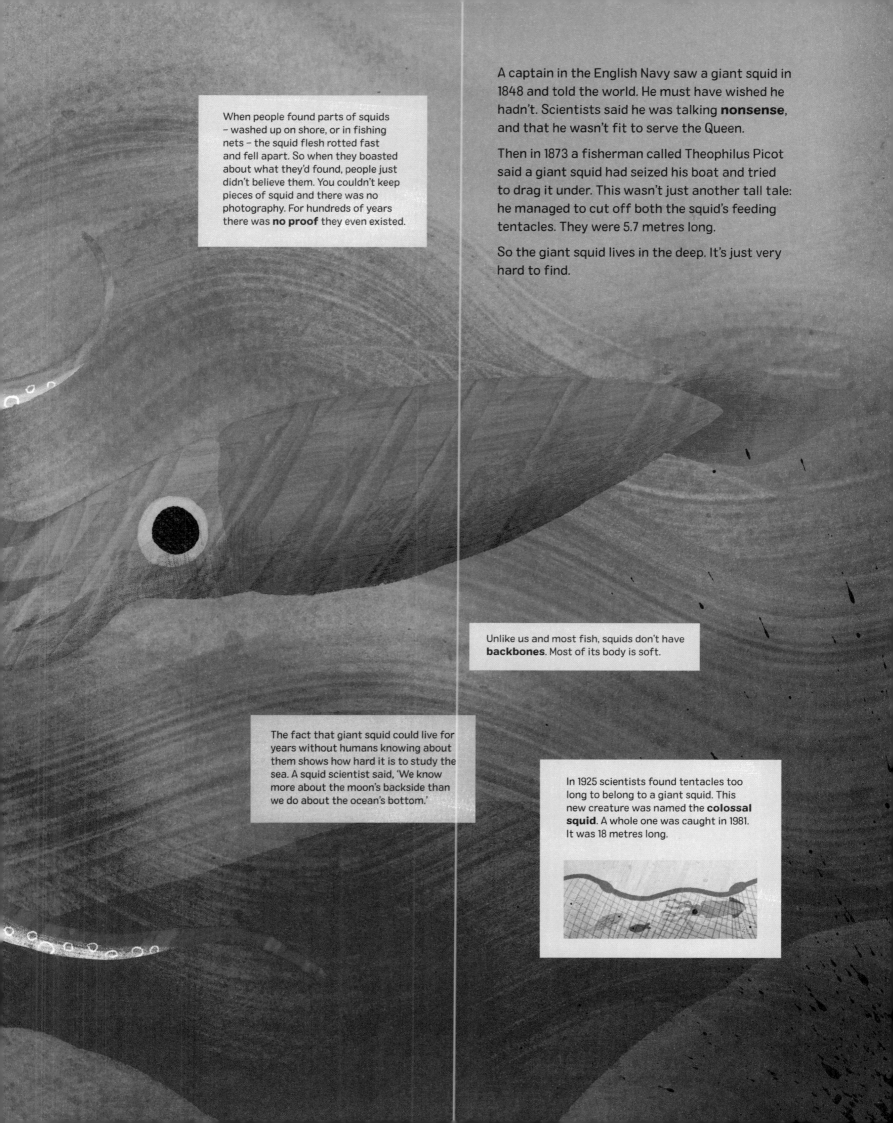

When people found parts of squids – washed up on shore, or in fishing nets – the squid flesh rotted fast and fell apart. So when they boasted about what they'd found, people just didn't believe them. You couldn't keep pieces of squid and there was no photography. For hundreds of years there was **no proof** they even existed.

A captain in the English Navy saw a giant squid in 1848 and told the world. He must have wished he hadn't. Scientists said he was talking **nonsense**, and that he wasn't fit to serve the Queen.

Then in 1873 a fisherman called Theophilus Picot said a giant squid had seized his boat and tried to drag it under. This wasn't just another tall tale: he managed to cut off both the squid's feeding tentacles. They were 5.7 metres long.

So the giant squid lives in the deep. It's just very hard to find.

Unlike us and most fish, squids don't have **backbones**. Most of its body is soft.

The fact that giant squid could live for years without humans knowing about them shows how hard it is to study the sea. A squid scientist said, 'We know more about the moon's backside than we do about the ocean's bottom.'

In 1925 scientists found tentacles too long to belong to a giant squid. This new creature was named the **colossal squid**. A whole one was caught in 1981. It was 18 metres long.

91 BEAVER

Beavers have been building, constructing and changing landscapes for thousands of years. Only humans have built more than beavers.

Like humans, beavers take on big building projects that change the areas where they live. They build **dams** across rivers and streams, and this alters the way the water flows. They build canals for moving branches. They build **lodges** to live in.

Sometimes this gets in the way of things humans want to build. Many beavers have been killed for that reason. But sometimes beavers can be a help to humans.

Humans have hunted beavers for their rich **fur** that keeps them warm in cold water, and also for a gland in their bodies that's used in medicine and perfumes.

When the first Europeans went to North America, there were about 90 million beavers there. By the late twentieth century, there were only between 6 and 12 million.

There are two species of beaver: American and European. They are **herbivores**, which means they only eat plants.

Beavers became extinct in the UK around 500 years ago, but now they have been brought back in a few places, such as **Devon** and **Scotland**.

Beavers build dams to make a place that suits them, where they can live safely and move the large pieces of tree they feed from. This creates watery **habitats** that many other plants and animals thrive in.

Beavers have returned to many parts of the USA. They have even been seen in New York City. They are also coming back in Europe.

The wetlands that beavers make help to hold water. This can help to stop **floods** when there is heavy rain.

GUANAY CORMORANT

Like all species of seabirds, the guanay cormorant must return to land to nest, and where there are lots of seabirds, there are lots of seabird droppings.

For over 1,500 years the people of South America gathered seabird droppings and put them on their fields. This made crops grow better. **Much better**.

When Europeans found out they wanted the bird droppings on their fields too. That way they could grow more food and so the droppings, called **guano**, became very valuable.

Guano changed the way humans lived. 12,000 years ago humans became farmers. Now people could farm **intensively**, which meant the world could feed more people.

Guano is full of stuff that plants need: nitrogen, phosphate, potassium. Scientists have learned how to make it from scratch, and we can now farm intensively all over the world without the help of the birds.

Alexander von Humboldt, a great German explorer, was in the docks in Peru when he started sneezing. His problem was a fine smelly dust. This was how Europeans first discovered guano.

The island of **Ichaboe** was found to be covered in a great hill of guano in 1843. The following year it was visited by 450 ships. When they had finished removing it the island was eight metres lower.

ICHABOE

In 1856, the USA claimed 100 islands where they could find guano. 70 of them are still owned by the USA today.

The nineteenth century has been called the **Age of Guano**: the way we farmed and grew our food was changed for ever.

93 MOUSE

We humans are a wasteful lot. We produce more food than we can eat. We throw away a lot of food that can still be eaten. So mice come and **share** it with us.

We didn't invite them, but mice are clever at hanging around humans, and at eating our food and rubbish.

They will eat almost anything. Like all rodents they are great **gnawers**: sometimes they gnaw through important electrical and computer cables and cause problems.

Mice can prove a real challenge to people. They pollute our food with their droppings and damage crops and buildings. To stop this, humans often try to kill mice with traps and poisons: but wherever there are humans you are likely to find mice, even in the **Antarctic**.

Mice can move very fast over short distances. They are terrific **jumpers** and are most active at night.

Some people are frightened of mice. But mice are often kept as pets, and their owners say they are **playful** and **affectionate**.

We brought cats into our homes to deal with mice. But there are many stories of clever mice **outwitting** cats. In the cartoons of *Tom and Jerry*, Jerry the mouse always gets the better of poor old Tom the cat.

Some scientists keep mice for **experiments**. Mice are the cheapest mammals for work in laboratories.

With their large round ears mice have good hearing and they also have an excellent sense of smell.

Mice have got onto seabird islands, where they eat the eggs and eat the chicks alive. It is very hard and very expensive to get rid of them.

94 STORK

Storks arrive in Europe in the spring. They make huge nests on houses and churches and live in what looks like perfect happiness. People even invented a pretty story about storks: that they bring **babies** to human families.

All summer and spring storks live around people, and then they go away in the winter. Many people wondered where they went. Did they sleep under the sea?

In 1822 a stork arrived in Germany with an arrow in its neck. The poor bird was then shot with a gun and people saw that the arrow had come from **Africa**. So they learned that the birds migrate to Africa for the winter.

There are **19 species** of storks. All of them are tall with big beaks.

Storks eat small animals, such as grasshoppers, frogs and mice.

Storks can travel for miles without flapping. Storks were the models for the first **gliders** that humans made.

The biggest species of stork is the **Marabou stork** that lives in Africa. Its wingspan can be up to 3.7 metres.

95 OYSTER

Oysters are good food that doesn't run away from you. Humans have been eating them for thousands of years.

When a piece of grit gets into an oyster, the oyster protects itself by covering the grit in a strong, iridescent material called nacre. It becomes a **pearl**, and pearls can be worth huge sums of money.

Natural pearls are rare. But these days oysters can be farmed. Put a bead in a farmed oyster and, a few months later, you'll have a pearl.

Many different kinds of shellfish are called oysters, even when they're not closely related to pearl oysters and edible oysters. These include **thorny**, **pilgrim**, **saddle** and **windowpane oysters**.

Seabed oysters protect seaside towns from big waves. They make underwater **barricades** that reduce the height of the waves.

Oysters clean the water they live in. Hundreds of litres pass through their bodies every day.

96 JAGUAR

We humans love big cats. We love jaguars not only because we find them beautiful, but because they tell us about an important idea.

The rainforest.

Jaguars live in America as far north as the southern United States. There are three places in South America where there are still a good few left. But mostly we think of jaguars as the animals of the **Amazon** rainforest.

Rainforests are important to us all. They are the Earth's **air-conditioning** system. They slow down the build-up of gases that make the world too hot, they give out water vapour that ends up as rain and they release oxygen into the world.

Rainforests are full of life: they cover 2 per cent of the Earth's surface and yet they hold more than **50 per cent** of the world's animal and plant species.

Jaguars are the world's biggest cats after lions and tigers. They live mostly on their own, or as a mother with cubs.

Jaguars are shorter than leopards, but stockier and stronger.

A jaguar's spots are arranged in **rosettes** and make different patterns to leopards.

Jaguars are **ambush predators**. They are good at hiding and sneaking up on their prey.

Jaguars are highly skilled at crawling, climbing and swimming.

Throughout this book we have looked at the way humans destroy things. Sometimes humans seem to be both stupid and mad. But we are also capable of acting with wisdom and generosity. We can do the right thing when we choose to: and that is the story of the pink pigeon.

Pink pigeons live on **Mauritius**, as the dodo once did. Unlike the dodo, they never quite became extinct – but in 1990 there were only **nine** pink pigeons left in the world.

This time people wanted to save them. The Mauritian Wildlife Foundation and the Durrell Wildlife Conservation Trust worked on a plan of action, and the number of pink pigeons started to rise again.

In 2018 there were 470 wild pink pigeons in the world. They were once Critically Endangered: now they are just **Vulnerable**. The pink pigeons are back.

The main problem facing pink pigeons was that the forests where they lived had been destroyed.

Pink pigeons also had difficulties with rats and other animals that had come to Mauritius with humans. These ate their eggs and the young pigeons in the nests.

There are now pink pigeons on a small island off the coast of Mauritius, called Ile aux Aigrettes, which has been cleared of rats.

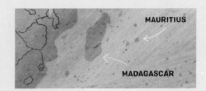

MAURITIUS

MADAGASCAR

The pink pigeon is a **herbivore** and likes to eat leaves, fruits, flowers and seeds.

But pink pigeons are not entirely safe. One disaster – like disease or a forest fire – could wipe out most of the population. You can never look at wildlife and believe that the job has been done.

98 VAQUITA

Vaquita is Spanish for little cow – but the animal is a **porpoise**, related to dolphins.

They live only in the Sea of Cortez off the coast of **Mexico**. The sea is roughly 1,100 kilometres long and is almost entirely surrounded by land.

Sadly, there's a fair chance that the vaquita will be the next large animal to become extinct. A survey in 2018 found there were only **12–15** vaquitas left in the world. That's not a lot of vaquitas. Saving the species will be a very hard job. But if we can save the pink pigeon, we might be able to save the vaquita too.

Vaquitas are about 1.4 metres long. They hunt for fish by using their voices to create **sound pictures** of their world.

Vaquitas get caught in fishing nets. It's against the law to leave these nets out, but the fishermen are poor and the fish they look for are **valuable**. When the vaquitas get caught in the nets, they often drown.

Vaquitas rarely dive deep. You can sometimes see them feeding with their backs exposed to the air.

Vaquitas share the Sea of Cortez with a fish called the **totoaba**. Some people will pay a lot of money for this fish. That's why some local people are so keen on catching it, even though it's against the law.

No one hates vaquitas – they just get in the way of people trying to make a living.

TERMITE/ANT

How many ants are there in the world?
10,000,000,000,000,000
(approximately ten thousand trillion).

In the twenty-first century, humans reached a tipping point. Most people on Earth now lived in crowded cities.

Ants and termites have been living very close together in the same sort of way for rather longer. They have been making and living in cities for about **120 million** years. They're much better at it than us.

Leafcutter ants take pieces of leaf into their nests and chew them up to make compost for growing **fungus**. They are farmers.

Some ants keep **aphids** because the aphids produce sticky stuff out of their bodies and the ants eat it. The ants herd the aphids, protect them and milk them. The aphids are like domestic animals.

Ants and termites make the system of intense togetherness work by specialising in different jobs and by doing things that are good for the whole **colony**, rather than the individual insect.

They have the most **complex** social lives on the planet – apart from us.

There are approximately **7.7 billion** humans in the world. That number is growing by 82 million a year.

When a lot of people live close together, they get anxious and stressed and ill. We're not as good at social living as ants and termites.

People do much better when they have some kind of nature to live with. Children learn better with outdoor lessons – especially those with learning difficulties and attention problems.

Ants can be found on every continent in the world, except for **Antarctica**.

100 POLAR BEAR

There's a famous painting of polar bears destroying the camp of a team of explorers. It's by Edwin Landseer, and it's called *Man Proposes, God Disposes*. The moral is that nature always beats humans in the end.

Now, nearly 200 years later, polar bears stand for the exact opposite: humans have beaten nature hands down – we are destroying the planet we live on.

The world is getting warmer and the ice around the North Pole is **melting**. The polar bear swimming endlessly across the sea in search of the vanished ice has brought that idea home to us.

We need to do something to **fix** this – and we need to do it now.

Polar bears are the world's largest land predator. They can weigh as much as three times the size of a lion. A big male polar bear can weigh up to 700 kilograms.

Polar bears hunt seals by sneaking up on them. They can smell a seal from 1.5 kilometres away.

Polar bears live in the Arctic Circle and love the cold. They start to overheat at 10 °C. The Earth is warmer by just over **1 °C** since 1880. That doesn't sound a lot, but it matters a great deal to the way the planet works.

The world overheated 251 million years ago and many animals and plants became extinct. The Earth recovered. But the snag is that it took millions of years.